Christ in Context

EUGENE TeSELLE
III

Christ
in Context

Divine Purpose and Human Possibility

FORTRESS PRESS
Philadelphia

Library of Congress Catalog Card Number 74-80426

ISBN 0-8006-0282-X

4404E74   Printed in U.S.A.   1-282

To Sallie

Table of Contents

Preface

This is an essay in advocacy, arguing against the Christo-centrist position that became popular in the theological world in recent years and in favor of another. I do it, however, as an admirer of Blondel and Teilhard, Barth and Rahner—the very thinkers whose position I am attacking—having been compelled by the drift of the problem to come to the opposite conclusion and wishing to save some of my favorite thinkers from the nonsense into which they were drawn and let the true implications of their views come forth.

Many who have been struck by the sudden decay of Christian conviction and theological seriousness during the past decade will be sure that I am only kicking a corpse, since theology, which had been kept artificially alive for some time, seems to have finally given up the ghost. But perhaps my awareness of the same features in the cultural scene has convinced me that the health of the theological enterprise demands forthright opposition to vague and inflated thinking. To be delivered from its occasional tendencies toward fantasy and subjectivism requires thinking critically and with real intent, taking difficulties seriously, assembling the evidence, working toward conclusions, always with an awareness of the problematical character of much that is said.

I have tried, therefore, to assemble a more or less ample dossier on this particular problem, beginning first, to set the question and give a certain authority to the thesis, with the New Testament and patristic literature. Then, to see what a "functional Christology" based on Jesus' relation to other men would involve and to explore some of its possible meanings, I have examined the classic period of German philosophy and theology. Finally, in order to drive home the necessity of my thesis and elaborate it, I have looked to our new evolutionary picture of the world. In retracing the course taken by Christian writers I have discovered how many subtleties there are to the problem and how many different perspectives there are to take on it. Therefore I hope that what is contained here will be read less as a historical report than as an initiation into a set of problems, an exploration of the considerations that must be heeded, and a more or less coherent development of a position. It is, I might say, a kind of preliminary sketch for a more constructive work in theology, probably long in the future; but what is here is probably audacious enough, both by treating traditional theological topics as though they are still worthy of consideration and by violating a number of the pieties of received theology (by which I mean the theology of the last few decades, read by anyone literate in the field).

There is little explicit discussion of Christology as such, the problem of the "person" of Christ. My concern is rather with the context of Christology, the set of relations within which it must be understood. It will become obvious, however, that I favor a Christology that stresses the humanity of Christ and, more than that, one that gives an important place to concrete human consciousness and development. At the same time I do not want to speak only of "the human Jesus" in such a way as to ignore the role of the divine Word, and even the "incarnation" or "condescension" or "relatedness" of the Word. But I would like to approach this latter theme in the manner of the Logos theology of the early centuries, not limiting the presence of the Word to the person of Jesus but seeing its signs everywhere in human life and the cosmos. In other words, I would like to go behind the christological controversies of the fifth century to the way of thinking that prevailed in earlier times and was brought to its fullest expression by Origen, a way of thinking in which the two "extreme" positions in Christology—divine relatedness to the world and presence in it, and fully human consciousness—can be held simultaneously.

Because the concern of this discussion is with the context and the different ways thinkers have approached it, I have been casual in my use of terminology and I can only plead that readers use good sense in interpreting it. The designations *Jesus* and *Christ* are usually used interchangeably, in accordance with conventional usage. When there seems to be a difference, "Jesus" refers to the personage accessible to (or at least sought by) historical study, or Jesus in his undeniable humanity, while "Christ" designates him as he is believed to be, or in his function in relation to others. The term *Christocentrism* is used to designate the position which I am attacking. Some may be offended at this, but in defense I would point out that the term is being used as a shorthand designation for the "Scotist" view that the incarnation is the center and aim of creation and of all God's activity toward the world. In attacking "Christocentrism" in this sense I am not denying it in some other senses; indeed, I shall myself be asserting that I am a Christocentrist "forward," with respect to the outworking of Jesus' influence in the world, but not "backward," with respect to God's purposes from the beginning. Finally I am pained at having to make too much use of the expression *man* in discussing the context in which Christ is interpreted, but the heritage of discussion is so full of terms like *Second Adam, Son of Man,* and *ideal man* that it has seemed less unwieldy simply to follow the idiom of less sensitive times.

The questions raised by contact with a number of laborers in the theological vineyard have been important to me through the years: H. Richard Niebuhr, who, in his usual searching way, raised questions about the "Unitarianism of the Son" which he found in Barth and others and insisted that every alternative be explored; Claude Welch, under whose guidance I made some of my first investigations in the nineteenth-century literature on the subject; Hans Frei, with whom I have had numerous conversations about these matters and who stimulated many reflections, perhaps through opposition as often as agreement; my fellow students and colleagues Peter Hodgson, David Kelsey, and John Schütz, with whom many undeveloped notions and prejudices were discussed; and a number of Vanderbilt students, especially David Fisher and Palmer Bell, who suggested or reacted to some of the formulations developed here. My wife Sallie, another fellow student and colleague, has been my most constant critic, stimulus, and support, and to her this book is dedicated with gratitude and love.

EUGENE TESELLE

The Divinity School
Vanderbilt University
October, 1974

Table of Abbreviations

Phen   G. W. F. Hegel, *The Phenomenology of Mind*, trans. J. M.
            Baillie, second edition (London: George Allen & Unwin,
            1931)

PL   *Patrologiae cursus completus. Series Latina*, ed. J.-B. Migne
            (Paris: Migne, 1844–64)

PR   Immanuel Kant, *Critique of Practical Reason*, trans. Lewis
            White Beck (New York: Liberal Arts Press, 1956) (cita-
            tions are given according to *AA* numberings)

Rel   Immanuel Kant, *Religion within the Limits of Reason Alone*,
            trans. Theodore M. Greene and Hoyt H. Hudson (LaSalle,
            Ind.: Open Court, 1934; reprinted Harper Torchbooks,
            1960)

SW   Friedrich Schleiermacher, *Sämmtliche Werke* (Berlin:
            Georg Reimer, 1836–64)

SW   F. W. J. von Schelling, *Sämmtliche Werke*, V (Stuttgart
            and Augsburg: Cotta, 1860)

SW   G. W. F. Hegel, *Sämmtliche Werke, Neue kritische Ausgabe*
            (Hamburg: Felix Meiner, 1952–   )

Werke   *Hegels Werke*, XIII (Berlin: Duncker und Humblot, 1832)

Introduction

In recent times it has come to be almost unquestioned dogma that the proper Christian view of the world is a Christocentric one. Such a position can be construed in different ways, of course: sometimes merely in an epistemological framework, viewing Jesus of Nazareth as the "paradigmatic event" in relation to which all events in human history are interpreted (the Niebuhrs); sometimes in an anthropological framework, viewing him as the center of the history of the human race (Schleiermacher); sometimes in an entire ontological framework, viewing him as the *raison d'être* of the entire cosmos insofar as theology is permitted to talk about it (Barth, Rahner). It is especially with the last of these that I wish to concern myself.

Christocentrism is not altogether a new development. It has gained fresh momentum, to be sure, from the attempts of modern theologians to meet the problem of knowledge by focusing upon an intra-mundane event and making it revelatory of the whole. But the tendency antedates these modern problems; it stems by lineal descent from Duns Scotus, who (perhaps because of epistemological problems of his own) took a forthright Christocentrist position, stating that the incarnation is the center and end of all God's activity in the world, that the incarnation, therefore, was not merely a remedy for sin but would have occurred even apart from sin, for its primary purpose was the fulfillment of the human race and of all creation.

Such a position, once put forth, seems to have held an irresistible appeal for theologians, especially the more impressionable, those who found aesthetic or intellectual pleasure in the harmoniousness of such a way of structuring the doctrines of the Church, for it does serve to bring everything into a unified pattern. It has been especially appealing to German theologians, perhaps because of some tantalizing similarities to the theosophy of Eckhart and Boehme and their many admirers, perhaps because of the strongly idealist and monist strand in German thought. In either case a cherished part of the heritage of German culture could be legitimated and Christianized. My own favorite among statements of that kind is Karl Rahner's dictum that God's first and comprehensive decision is that in which "the divine Logos comes to exist in the emptiness of that which is not God" (*"der Logos Gottes in der Leere des Aussergöttlichen ek-sistieren wird"*).[1] The whole counsel of God can then be understood from this one event, and the creation of the human race, even of the cosmos as a whole, are merely the indispensable preconditions for the fulfillment of this all-comprehending purpose.

In the face of near unanimity among modern theologians I wish to file a dissenting report. Precisely because Christocentrism has come to be so widely held that theologians cannot conceive themselves doing without it, the assumption must be examined carefully lest a new dogma arise almost by inadvertence. The outcome, I might say in advance, will not be a total rejection of the position; but it does seem to me that its insights break down into several components which, properly understood, do *not* coalesce into what is commonly meant by Christocentrism. Even if the Christian has apostolic warrant for attempting to discern the hidden wisdom of God (1 Cor. 2:6–13), the result may be more complex than the one put forward by the modern doctors of Christocentrism.

An alternative hypothesis against which to pit it is not hard to find. It is already extant in the position taken by nearly all of the fathers, the scholastics, and the theologians of the Reformation and Tridentine era. Epistemologically, the figure of Jesus is *not* regarded as the sole source of our knowledge of God, for a considerable confidence is placed in the possibilities of general knowledge. Thus theology is not locked up within the Christian consciousness but can move out into the broader world of human experience. Anthropologically, the uniqueness and indispensability of Jesus are understood not primarily in relation to human fulfillment but in relation to sin. To the fathers and the scholastics it was beyond question that apart from sin the incarnation would *not* have occurred, because it would not have been needed, and conse-

1. "Zur Theologie der Gnade," *Theologische Quartalschrift*, CXXXVIII (1958): 71 (*Theological Investigations*, IV, 213).

quently that a right relation to God is possible, at least under conditions of sinlessness, without Christ. Ontologically, they did not think that the incarnation is the key to the existence and the character of the created world, at least when we are looking backward toward the origins of things. (Once sin has taken place and the destiny of the human race and the world is linked to the Redeemer, the situation is, of course, quite different.)

The crucial question, then, is whether the status of Christ is such as to claim a unique position of dominance in organizing the work of theology. To many practitioners of the discipline in modern times, contrary to what one might have expected in an age of disciplined and often skeptical study of the biblical heritage, it has been unthinkable to deny it—perhaps because the problems of knowledge and of method were so intense as to drive them more deeply within the circle of faith. But to most of the theologians of the past, contrary once again to what one might have expected from an age of faith, it was quite thinkable to give the human figure of Jesus a strictly delimited function—perhaps because they had a more sanguine confidence in the broader experiences and reflections of men and women.

It is apparent that a direct clash of sensibilities will occur, with abundant possibilities for caricature and invective from both sides. The Christocentrist approach, in whatever form, strives toward organic unity, and the organizing principle around which all else is structured is something that is not generally accessible, something particular, indeed unique. Preeminence is given in every way to Christ, and the independent validity of other standpoints is brought under suspicion if not rejected outright. The alternative approach is prepared to give to the figure of Jesus a *delimited* position and function within the subject-matter of theology: not all that is said about man need be linked immediately to Christology, not all that is seen in the cosmos need be directed toward Christ, not all reflection need be carried on within the circle of faith. From this perspective the Christocentrist position always has a tinge of Gnosticism, an appeal to privileged communications which are not accessible to others, a failure to meet the challenge to relate revelation and reason.

In view of the prestige of Christocentrism and its rhetorical advantages, engulfing everything, as it does, in the atmosphere of Christian piety, the case for the alternative position must be assembled with care. Let us consider, then, three major phases in the discussion of the problem.

First there is the traditional phase, extending from the New Testament through the patristic and scholastic periods and on into the era of Reformation and Counter-Reformation. An examination of this phase not only will furnish a foundation in authority and precedent for the position I want to develop but will rough out all the basic points that must be made. But we should not expect more than a "roughing out." We shall find only shards, fragmentary discussions of the problem as it happens to arise, usually only by the way, in connection with other topics, occasionally more explicitly, but even then as one out of many scholastic questions.

Next there is the creative period of modern German theology during which Kant and Schleiermacher and Hegel and their many followers, newly aware of the problematical character of both authority and reason, tried to place Christology on a new footing, in terms of general human experience and the universal human situation before God. In retracing the course of their inquiries we shall learn much about the difficulties of thinking about Christ and gaining certitude about him; but we shall also discover that the game is far from lost and that it is possible to devise, on the basis of a critical examination of the human situation, a framework of meanings, a way of thinking and speaking, which can be utilized for christological assertions, although it will not, by itself, furnish the content of those assertions except in a schematic way.

Finally we must examine the evolutionary understanding of the world—usually called to the aid of the Christocentrist perspective—and take note of the restrictions it places upon what the Christian says about God's purposes, restrictions which actually make the Christocentrist position impossible. The reader will discover that I really deal quite gently and sympathetically with the Christocentrists of our own time, for the most noted among them—Blondel, Teilhard, Barth, Rahner—are precisely those thinkers whom I most admire for directly confronting modern problems and trying to show that the Christian faith need not stand in terror of them. But it is more important to follow the process of their thinking than to quote slavishly the statements that have come out of it. It seems to me that what is implied by the problems they investigate, even by their own general perspective on God's relation to the world, is *not* the Christocentrism they have championed but an intensified version of the more traditional position.

We shall be looking, then, first at the problem and its early history; then at an important series of explorations of the language and conceptual framework that might be used to address it; and finally at the current state of the question, as best it can be puzzled out. Because of their differences in subject matter and place in the argument, each chapter will be of a different genre and tonality. The first will be a historical overview tracing the development of the question and showing the support given by traditional thought to the thesis I want to argue. The second will be an exercise in discovering how a coherent answer might be given, how a conceptual framework might be devised for making assertions about the relation of Christ to human history. The third will be assertive, driving home the necessity of taking this position and elaborating it in contemporary terms.

The first two chapters, then, while historical, are also part of a constructive theological argument, and the subject matter has been selected not in a purely historical way but because of its pertinence to the argument, either as giving backing to or offering insights into the position I am taking, or as casting doubt upon or posing difficulties to the alternative view. It should be noted, however, that not everything in these chapters will necessarily build the argument. In part this will be because the negative considerations, while they can count against the alternative, may not always suggest as much about the position that is being developed. But it is chiefly because these first two chapters are, after all, historical in their scope, and I want to resist the kind of interpretation of writings from the past that seeks direct, one-to-one contributions to current discussion. What these chapters can do is to show us how the same general problem was discussed in several different settings, with different assumptions, and so induce us to think the problem through with them once again, respecting their distance from ourselves as well as the similarities in their concerns. This, to me, is the character of any proper "historical theology." But in the process we shall also find ourselves being initiated into new ways of approaching the question, and I hope that the overall force of the investigation will be to move toward and prepare the way for the points that are made in the concluding chapter.

CHAPTER I

The Emergence of the Question

First let us look at the heritage of Christian thought, not solely for the purpose of arguing, on the basis of authority and precedent, that the extreme "Christocentrist" position is out of bounds but also in order to see how the question came gradually to be formulated and discussed. (For the Christocentrist position *was* attested from time to time through the centuries, and good arguments based on time-honored Christian principles can be given in favor of it.) We must not expect too much. The discussion was at best fragmentary, and mostly we shall be examining assumptions or piecing together isolated comments. But even under these limitations the result, I think, will be instructive.

What we shall find, simply by working inductively, is that three basic assumptions were held, each of them contrary to the assertions of the Christocentrist position: (1) that the significance of Jesus lies chiefly in his renewed humanity, bringing to fulfillment a possibility or destiny that was laid before human life from the first; (2) that the divine Word can without question be present and knowable before and apart from the incarnation, even before and apart from any historical revelation, and (3) that the incarnation, like the whole history of salvation, is part of God's purpose only because of his (fore) knowledge of what persons will do in their freedom. The assumptions can be taken up separately, and in this order, because the major statements in which they are expressed come from different writers, in a rough chronological sequence. Then we shall come to the discussion, pro and con, of the Christocentrist thesis, which became explicit only during the period of scholastic theology and forms the immediate background of the nineteenth- and twentieth-century reflection along these lines.

7

I. Jesus as the New Man

When we come to the New Testament asking about its characterization of the role of Jesus in relation to other men, we ought to be surprised at what it does *not* stress—Jesus' proclamation of the kingdom of
God and his own relation to it, or the early Church's proclamation of
Jesus as Messiah or Lord, or the various suggestions that Jesus is to be
placed in continuity with Moses and the prophets and the righteous
men of the past. All these themes are present, of course; but whatever
the reason—perhaps they were too "Hebraic" for an increasingly Hel-
lenized Christianity, perhaps they were subject to misunderstanding on
other grounds—they do not become the core around which early Christian reflection for the most part crystallizes. Instead we must look to
Paul's reflections about Jesus as the "New Adam," the forerunner of a
renewed humanity—not as though they contain the whole of Pauline
or New Testament Christology, or exhaust the importance of Christ to
others, but in order to see how Paul traces the connections between
Christ and the broader life of the human race.

The scholars have long suspected that Paul's Second Adam doctrine
is connected with the Son of Man theme found in the gospel tradition.[1]
For our purposes it is enough to note the probability that both themes
were derived, by routes which it is difficult to trace, from Iranian and
Hellenistic speculations about the Original Man and the hoped-for res-
toration of humanity to its primal state. In most Jewish speculation, as
Cullmann points out, there was a tendency to deny Adam's sin (blam-
ing it instead upon Eve, or upon Satan) and to establish a link, sometimes even an identity, between Adam and the redeeming Son of Man.
This tendency is continued in some of the early Christian literature,
especially the Odes of Solomon and the pseudo-Clementines, and it
meshes neatly with the Gnostic doctrine that man's redemption is
accomplished through gaining awareness of his inmost, truest self. But
there could also be a counter tendency to set up a contrast between
Adam and the transcendent Man. At least we know that Philo distinguished between Adam, "formed from dust," and the human being

---

1. See especially Oscar Cullmann, *The Christology of the New Testament*, trans.
Shirley Guthrie and Charles A. M. Hall (Philadelphia: Westminster Press, 1959),
pp. 144–51, 166–81; Matthew Black, "The Pauline Doctrine of the Second
Adam," *Scottish Journal of Theology*, VII (1954): 170–79; and Edvin Larsson,
*Christus als Vorbild. Eine Untersuchung zu den paulinischen Tauf- und Eikontex-
ten* (Acta Seminarii Neotestamentici Upsaliensis, XXIII; Uppsala: C. W. K. Glee-
rup, 1962), pp. 239–40, 255, 313–14.

(male and female together) created "after God's image," either in order to differentiate actual from ideal man or, when he linked the two, in order to emphasize that the highest aspect of man is breathed into him by God and partakes of the divine Logos.[2] It is in the setting of speculations like these that Paul reflected upon the place of Jesus in the universal history of sin and salvation. Like Philo he seems concerned to set up a contrast between Adam and true humanity; but unlike Philo (or the Gnostics), he looks for this true humanity not in a heavenly model, and not in a divine spirit which is central to each person, but only at the dawning of the last times, in Jesus, the Last Adam who is the first to be in any unequivocal sense the "image of God."[3]

We may start with Rom. 5:12–21, the most explicit paralleling of Adam and Christ. Sin, Paul is saying, came into the world through one man, Adam, and spread to all men—not by hereditary transmission, but through their being in a common situation, that which is described in Rom. 1:18–23, having sufficient awareness of God to be capable of acknowledging and glorifying him, but failing at the task and showing themselves to be fully culpable. Not only sin but death spreads to all men, "inasmuch as (*eph' hōi*) all men sinned," even when their sins were *not* like Adam's sin. Now in all of this, Paul suggests, Adam is shown to be a *typos*—perhaps a prefiguration, perhaps a pattern, perhaps a mere shadow—of the one to come (5:14). The force of the parallel is spelled out a few verses later. Just as one man's disobedience led to condemnation for all, one man's obedience leads to justification and life for all (5:18 and 20). In other words, both Adam and Christ are in a position to shape the destiny of the many who are associated with them, those who are, respectively, "in Adam" (in the corporate life of a sinful humanity) and "in Christ" (in the community of salvation); but in neither case is individual responsibility denied to the others.

2. Jacob Jervell, *Imago Dei. Gen. 1: 26f. im Spätjudentum, in der Gnosis und in den paulinischen Briefen* (Forschungen zur Religion and Literatur des Alten und Neuen Testaments, N.F. LVIII; Göttingen: Vandenhoeck and Ruprecht, 1960), pp. 55, 59–60, 64–66.

3. For general surveys of Paul's views on this topic, see, in addition to those already mentioned, W. D. Davies, *Paul and Rabbinic Judaism* (second edition, London: S.P.C.K., 1955), chap. 3; C. K. Barrett, *From First Adam to Last: A Study in Pauline Theology* (London: Adam & Charles Black, 1962); Robin Scroggs, *The Last Adam: A Study in Pauline Anthropology* (Philadelphia: Fortress Press, 1966); and John G. Gibbs, *Creation and Redemption: A Study in Pauline Theology* (Supplements to Novum Testamentum, XXVI; Leiden: Brill, 1971).

There is, then, this similarity of function between Adam and Christ. But Paul simultaneously stresses the contrast between their acts and between the consequences of those acts. If the transgression of Adam was the occasion of sin for many, the grace of God and its free gift in Christ have overflowed abundantly for many; if the consequence of the one act is their being ruled over by sin and death, the consequence of the grace of God is justification and their being made to rule in fullness of life (5:15–17). The difference consists not only in the antithesis between disobedience and obedience, but even more in the superior dignity and power of the second. If the one had such momentous influence in human life, "how much more" will the acts of the second Adam and the grace of the Spirit have power for redeeming them (5:15); "where sin increased, grace abounded all the more" (5:20). The contrast, then, is in the last analysis between the fundamental weakness of sin—initiated without foresight of the consequences, perpetuated through passivity toward past transgressions—and the purposeful action of the grace of God.[4]

In 1 Cor. 15:20–28 and 42–57, we find the same parallel—and antithesis—between Adam and Christ, but this time with a more comprehensive field of vision, for here Paul has under consideration not only the contrast between sin and renewal within earthly history but the even more drastic tension between death and resurrection. Since the entire passage is motivated by Paul's attack upon those who are claiming to be already victorious over death (1 Cor. 15:12–19 and 29–34), he stresses that it is *the dead* who are raised to incorruption, and he anchors his argument in the twin extremes of creation and eschaton.

> Thus it is written, "The first man Adam became a living being"; the last Adam became a life-giving spirit. But it is not the spiritual which is first but the physical, and then the spiritual. The first man was from the earth, a man of dust; the second man is from heaven. As was the man of dust, so are those who are of the dust; and as is the man of heaven, so are those who are of heaven. Just as we have borne the image of the man of dust, we shall also bear the image of the man of heaven. (15:45–49)

---

4. This point is made well by Karl Barth, *Christ and Adam: Man and Humanity in Romans 5* (New York: Harper & Row, 1957), pp. 44–60, despite the excessively Christocentrist bias that dominates his interpretation as a whole.

Here the "last man" is "the man of heaven," Christ after his exaltation. His importance for others continues, then, beyond his obedience and suffering on earth, and he becomes the basis and guarantee of what others are destined to become.

Why the definite sequence, "first the physical, then the spiritual"? It could mean that Christ, in the process of repairing the damage done by sin, does not merely restore humanity to its original state but effects a further growth, first in himself and then in others—a growth which had scarcely begun in Adam when it was inhibited and distorted by sin but is now begun afresh as a "new creation" (Gal. 6:15; 1. Cor. 7:31) and can now progress, though through constant struggle, toward its fulfillment in the eschaton. But even more seems to be involved than a "progress" of this sort. Linking 1 Corinthians 15 with Romans 5 we see that the "earthly" or the "physical" is bound up with sin and death, perhaps as their effect, perhaps as occasioning them (interpreters of Paul have fought with each other over this question, but on either hypothesis the result is the same). The reason the "heavenly man" must come later in time—indeed, the reason he must "come" at all—is that the children of Adam remain permanently under the law of sin and death. Therefore the way to a new creation necessarily goes through death first and then resurrection, calling for resources that are not available to the earthly Adam and can be gained only through following the way of Christ.[5] Thus the stakes are raised. The question is not merely one of sin and renewal; it concerns ultimate fulfillment or the lack of it:

> For as by a man came death, by a man has come also the resurrection of the dead. For as in Adam all die, so also in Christ shall all be made alive. (15:21–22)

Eschatological perfection, called "life" or "glory," is the focus toward which all of Pauline thought converges; but it glimpses that focal point only across the abyss of death and resurrection.

Christ does have a unique and indispensable function, then, since it is only with and through him that others reach fulfillment. He is the

5. Larsson especially points up the role of *death* in determining this "first . . . then" (pp. 314–15) and suggests that Paul was influenced by both the traditions in Jewish thought, both that which ascribed mortality to Adam's creation out of dust and that which ascribed it to sin (pp. 315–19).

only one of whom Paul can say unambiguously that he "is the image of God" (2 Cor. 4:4). But this is a bothersome identification, since its meaning is not so clear as we might at first suppose. It could mean that Christ is what Adam was, and ceased to be; or that he comes up to the full measure of what Adam should have become; or, if we take seriously the possibility that Paul, like Philo, differentiated between man "formed from dust" and man "after God's image," that he is the one who for the first time brings humanity to its originally intended destiny. When we recall that the Greek translation of Gen. 1:27 read "*after* God's image," leading Philo, and Origen and Athanasius after him, to suppose that man is only a copy of the *true* Image, the divine Logos, then another possibility must also be added, that Paul is here thinking of Christ as that divine Image "after which" Adam was created.[6] This last interpretation falls to the ground, however, when we remember Paul's notorious *obiter dictum* in the controversy over the covering of heads during worship and note that he could say, in a most un-Philonic way, that man "is the image and glory of God; but woman is the glory of man" (1 Cor. 11:7). Paul must be credited with reading Hebrew and not being bullied by the Greek text. We can safely interpret his statements as referring to Christ in his humanity, and probably in the sense that he exhibits *for the first time* humanity as it was intended to be.

His significance for others is described in a number of passages which play on the notion of *image*. "Just as we have borne the image of the man of dust" (with his undeveloped beginnings and the dysfunction of sin), "we shall also bear the image of the man of heaven" (1 Cor. 15:49); God has "predestined" them "to be conformed to the image of his Son" (Rom. 8:29); they "are being changed into his likeness from one degree of glory to another, for this comes from the Lord who is the Spirit" (2 Cor. 3:18); Christ is being "formed" in them (Gal. 4:19); Christ "will change" their bodies "to be like his glorious body" (Phil. 3:21). Yet his function as "image of God" is not jealously protected; rather he is the prototype, the real model in accordance with which, and by whose influence, others are to be formed. He is

6. This is the thesis of Jervell (pp. 217, 276, etc.) and of Matthew Black and others before him. It can invoke in its support the use of "image of God" in Col. 1:15, but since the Pauline origin of that passage is disputed it cannot be made the basis of a judgment about Paul's general doctrine.

"the first-born among *many* brethren" (Rom. 8:29); they are "*fellow* heirs" with him (Rom. 8:17); he is the "first fruits" of those who have been subjected to death, but he is to be followed by many *others* (1 Cor. 15:20 and 23); the *whole* creation (or just possibly "the whole creature," man in all aspects, body, soul, and spirit) sighs with longing for liberation from bondage to decay, and even those who have the Spirit likewise groan in travail, awaiting the fulfillment which will come only in resurrection (Rom. 8:19–23); Christ's unique role as "Lord" (Ps. 110:1) is exercised as the representative of *humanity* (Ps. 8:7), under which all is to be placed in subjection (1 Cor. 15:25–27; cf. Heb. 2:5–9); and his role will *cease* when his work of overcoming the enemies of humanity is finished, for then God will be "all in all." (1 Cor. 15:28).

In order to be sure of this interpretation of Paul—and to understand the precise qualifications he wants to make—we must look closely at the one passage in which Christ is identified explicitly as "the image of God" (2 Cor. 4:4), and since it is a difficult passage we must take into account the entire context, 2 Cor. 3:1–4, 6.[7] Paul is in the process of defending his authority as an apostle against rivals who have come bearing letters of certification. This leads him into a complex discussion of the difference between the ministry of the "old covenant" (or better, the "ancient" or "classic" covenant, since this is what the Greek term *palaia* would have connoted) and the "new covenant" (really the same covenant renewed)—between the ministry of condemnation, which operates through the law written on tablets of stone, and the ministry of reconciliation with God, in which the same law is written on human hearts by the Spirit. The extended allegory on the veil that Moses put over his face when the Israelites could not endure to behold its splendor (Exodus 34) does not seem to be called for by the context. It seems rather to be an intrusion, full of logical and grammatical anomalies and connected only tenuously to what goes before and after. Therefore many commentators have suggested that it recollects an earlier Jewish tradition of exegesis, and that Paul introduces it not as his own "midrash" to clarify the point he is making but rather as a polemi-

---

7. I would refer the reader to the commentaries, and especially to Karl Prümm, *Diakonia Pneumatos. Der zweite Korintherbrief als Zugang zur apostolischen Botschaft.* Band I. *Theologische Auslegung des zweiten Korintherbriefs* (Rome-Freiburg-Vienna: Herder, 1967), pp. 97–227.

cal alternative to an interpretation already being put forward by his opponents. This would be in keeping with the character of the letter as a whole, for it is argumentative from first to last, directed against some new Christian teachers who had come into Corinth.[8]

The most likely possibility is that these opponents thought of Jesus as a kind of new Moses, for this was a common tendency in Jewish Christianity, and Paul does speak of them as "Hebrews, Israelites, sons of Abraham" (2 Cor. 11:22). But since the opponents with whom he is concerned in this letter are not Judaizers of the sort we encounter in the letter to the Galatians but seem rather to have made much of their spiritual qualities, their wisdom, their abilty to work wonders, they must have been Hellenistic Jews, strongly influenced by the religious and intellectual milieu of the Greek world before their conversion to Christianity. Georgi shows that all the data fit together if we suppose their thinking to have centered around the Hellenistic notion of the *theios anēr*, the man who is filled with the divine Spirit and partakes of divine qualities. Moses would be such a man, and so would Christ, in the supreme degree. Paul's opponents could also claim similar things for themselves, in dependence upon Christ, of course, but sharing the same qualities exhibited by him. What we would have, then, is a Christology stressing the divine Spirit that indwelt Jesus in the highest degree, but also Moses and the prophets in the past, and now these "superlative apostles" (2 Cor. 11:5) and the entire fellowship of the Church in the present. Such a Christology, it will be noted, is not entirely unfamiliar, for we have seen many unconscious approximations to it through the centuries. It is not without religious appeal. Yet Paul objects to the claims that these "superlative apostles" make for themselves, and says that they preach a different Jesus, a different Spirit, a different gospel (2 Cor. 11:4). Why?

The problem is that they preach an earthly Jesus, a Christ "after the flesh" (5:16), in other words, a *theios anēr*, a wonder-worker and charismatic teacher of wisdom, while Paul finds instead discontinuity,

---

8. See Siegfried Schulz, "Die Decke des Moses. Untersuchungen zu einer vorpaulinischen Überlieferung," *Zeitschrift für die neutestamentliche Wissenschaft*, XLIX (1958): 1–30, esp. 21–27; and Dieter Georgi, *Die Gegner des Paulus im 2. Korintherbrief. Studien zur religiösen Propaganda in der Spätantike* (Wissenschaftliche Monographien zum alten und neuen Testament, XI; Neukirchen: Neukirchener Verlag, 1964), pp. 246–92.

in Jesus and in himself as an apostle and in every believer, between the earthly state of humility and the heavenly state of exaltation.[9] They will disagree, then, at every point, even when they want to affirm many of the same things.

Now we are ready to look at the tension between their two ways of reading the passage from Exodus concerning Moses' veil. These Hellenizing Jews could well have interpreted it, Georgi shows, as a symbol of the relationship between the external letter of Scripture (or other modes of expression, such as speech) and the inward presence of the divine Spirit. The external medium conceals an allegorical meaning and spiritual power, both restraining men from making too quick an approach and preparing them for an eventual direct encounter. Thus Moses, and *a fortiori* Christ, whose inward splendor was even greater, would not attempt to lead men immediately to the same kind of direct encounter with the divine Spirit that they enjoyed but would rather communicate with them through words and instruct them in ways they were capable of understanding. Then, when they were ready, they could follow the example of Moses, for when he turned to the Lord, he removed the veil (Exod. 34:34; 2 Cor. 3:16). The exegetical comment that follows, "The Lord [who is mentioned here] is the Spirit" (3:17), would also fit into that same pre-Pauline interpretation, as an explanation that the hidden meaning of this passage is that every person should turn from the outward letter to the Spirit which is within him. The climax of that interpretation, then, would be the statement, "And we, beholding the glory of the Lord [=the Spirit] with unveiled faces, are being transformed from glory to glory, as is befitting of the Lord who is the Spirit" (3:18).[10]

Paul's objection—and this is clearly in line with other passages in the letter—would be that they postulate too much of a continuity between Moses, Christ, and themselves, attempting a direct *imitatio Christi*, to the extent, perhaps, of teaching in veiled, allegorical statements of their own, like those ascribed to Moses and doubtless to Christ as well (4:2–3; cf. 3:12–13). Paul wishes instead to establish a discontinuity

9. Cf. Georgi, *Die Gegner des Paulus*, pp. 284–87.
10. See the tentative reconstruction of the pre-Pauline *Vorlage* in Georgi, p. 282. I have retained a few more details than Georgi has, for reasons that seem entirely solid to me.

between the ancient dispensation and the new: the former is one of condemnation, the latter one of justification. While it was quite appropriate in the former for spiritual truth to be veiled—indeed, to such an extent that the veil remains and, far from becoming transparent to the truth, lies as a pall over their hearts (3:15)—in the latter there is an open and straightforward proclamation of the truth (3:12; 4:2). Paul wishes also to establish a discontinuity between Christ and his followers. The claim of the rival apostles to be in succession to Christ, and to be able to prove this from their spiritual virtuosity and their letters of certification, is a relapse into a religion of the letter and an apostleship that is of men rather than God (cf. also Gal. 1:10–17 and 3:1–4).

Therefore Paul step by step destroys the mysticism of his opponents, according to which the light of the Spirit falls upon the unveiled heart of each person. Abandoning the imagery of veiling and unveiling through mystical vision, he attributes illumination only to the apostolic message, the gospel, which alone manifests the glory of God which shines in the face of Jesus Christ (4:4 and 6). The Spirit is not forgotten; but it becomes the Spirit of Christ, made present with and through the gospel. Thus everything remains dependent upon the human figure of Jesus, who alone can be called without reservation "the image of God" (4:4). Any participation by others in his qualities will come not through imitating him and turning directly to the Spirit, but through hearing the gospel from the apostles and receiving the Spirit that comes from him. It is only then, and under those conditions, that they will be "beholding the glory of the Lord" and "changed into his likeness from one degree of glory to another" (2 Cor. 3:18), and even this transformation is only in the "inner nature" (4:16–17), a looking toward eternal glory from out of the midst of earthly struggle.[11]

There is one more passage that we must examine in connection with the Pauline theme of the New Adam. This is Phil. 2:5–11, the last to be

11. This is, of course, a point often made about Paul, but its polemical force against other types of early Christian thinking has only recently been brought out. See, for example, Ernst Käsemann, "The Beginnings of Christian Theology," *Journal for Theology and the Church*, VI (1969): 42–43, where the tension between an uncontrolled post-resurrection enthusiasm and the definiteness of the gospel, centered entirely in Christ, is noted; and especially James M. Robinson and Helmut Koester, *Trajectories through Early Christianity* (Philadelphia: Fortress Press, 1971), chaps. 2 and 6, where the different trends within early Christianity are classified and their consequences are exposed.

written and without doubt the most difficult to interpret.[12] "Have this mind [disposition] among yourselves which you have in Christ Jesus," Paul begins; and then, probably quoting a pre-Pauline hymn,[13] he goes on:

6 He, being originally in the form of God
  did not count it booty
  to be as God,

7 But emptied himself,
  taking the form of a slave,
  being changed in the likeness of men.

8 And finding himself, in fashion, like a man,
  he humbled himself,
  becoming obedient unto death.

9 Therefore God has highly exalted him
  and given him the name
  that is above every name,

10 That at the name of Jesus
  every knee should bow,
  in heaven and on earth and under the earth,

11 And every tongue confess,
  "Jesus Christ is Lord,"
  to the glory of God the Father.

The customary interpretation, of course, is that the referent of the opening strophes is the divine Word, the second person of the Trinity. But there is a minority viewpoint through the centuries, not to be

12. Although I disagree with its conclusions in almost every detail, I would refer the reader, for a thorough discussion of the problems and a review of the literature, to R. P. Martin, *Carmen Christi: Philippians ii. 5–11 in Recent Interpretation and in the Setting of Early Christian Worship* (Cambridge: Cambridge University Press, 1967). A crucial contribution to recent scholarship is Ernst Käsemann, "Kritische Analyse von Phil. 2, 5–11," *Zeitschrift für Theologie und Kirche*, XLVII (1950): 313–60, reprinted in *Exegetische Versuche und Besinnungen*, I (Göttingen: Vandenhoeck und Ruprecht, 1960), 51–95. Note should also be taken of the wealth of grammatical analysis and the survey of the history of exegesis in Paul Henry, "Kénose," *Dictionnaire de la Bible, Supplément*, V (1957): 7–161. The most recent discussion is Jack T. Sanders, *The New Testament Christological Hymns: Their Historical Religious Background* (Cambridge: Cambridge University Press, 1971), chap. 3 and the summary remarks on pp. 96–98, which suggest that here as elsewhere we are faced with a "developing myth" or an "emerging mythical configuration" drawing upon a number of distinct motifs.

13. Ernst Lohmeyer, *Kyrios Jesus. Eine Untersuchung zu Phil. 2, 5–11* (Sitzungsberichte der Heidelberger Akademie der Wissenschaften, Phil.-hist. Klasse, Jahrgang 1927–28, 4. Abhandlung; Heidelberg, 1928); also *Die Brief an die Philipper* ("Meyer Kommentar"; Göttingen: Vandenhoeck und Ruprecht, 1930).

ignored, which holds that the referent is Jesus as a finite subject who freely elects to share the destiny of sinful men. Some decades ago Friedrich Loofs canvassed the patristic texts; although he exhibited a certain carelessness about the subtleties, he did make a persuasive case that this latter interpretation is the earliest and the most in keeping with Paul, and that the alternative interpretation was of Gnostic origin and tendency.[14] Although Loofs, like most other historians, does not seem to recognize it, the same view is also found in Origen, who believed that all human minds have existed since their creation in eternity, and that the mind called "Christ" is the only one that adhered to the Logos without falling away. Being a subtle and generally sincere exegete, he saw that the Philippians passage reinforced his theory: this mind, which had been "in the form of God" (resembling God because of intimate knowledge and fervent will) later took on "the form of a slave" for the sake of sinful men.[15] This interpretation of the passage was then submerged for many centuries, until it was reasserted by the Lutheran theologians in a different way again. They stressed the communion of the two natures in Christ (especially in defense of their eucharistic doctrine) to such an extent as to assert that the humanity took on the attributes of divinity from the first moment of incarnation, and that it was only the self-emptying (*kenōsis, exinanitio*) of the incarnate Word that gave to Jesus his ordinary human characteristics.[16]

These are only straws in the wind; they are too much governed by later theological notions to be reliable historical interpretations of Paul or the pre-Pauline hymnodist. They do indicate, nonetheless, that the passage has suggested to a variety of readers a different meaning than that commonly given to it, and even their disagreements over the details put us on warning that the passage will not be easy to interpret.

---

14. "Das altkirchliche Zeugnis gegen die herrschende Auffassung der Kenosisstelle (Phil. 2, 5–11)," *Theologische Texte und Untersuchungen*, C (1927–28): 1–102.

15. This is attested by Jerome, *Apol.*, II, 12; Theophilus of Alexandria, *Ep. syn.*, 4; and the seventh and twelfth anathemas of the Second Council of Constantinople. See the notes by G. W. Butterworth in his translation of *Origen on First Principles* (London: S.P.C.K., 1936), p. 250, n. 3, and p. 320, n. 1.

16. *Formula of Concord*, Epitome, VIII, 11; Solid Declaration, VIII, 26. For the discussion of this doctrine among the Lutheran theologians see Heinrich Schmid, *The Doctrinal Theology of the Evangelical Lutheran Church*, third edition, trans. Charles A. Hay and Henry E. Jacobs (Philadelphia: Luther Publication Society, 1899; Minneapolis: Augsburg Publishing House, 1961), pp. 381–94.

I am prepared to acknowledge, in fact, that there is a systematic ambiguity about the whole passage. It is finally impossible to prove conclusively whether it refers to the divine Logos, or to a lesser preexistent being (divine, angelic, or human), or to the earthly Jesus, although I am inclined toward the last, for reasons that will be made clear. Not everything in Paul's Christology hangs on this passage. The only question is whether it should be listed among his characterizations of Christ as the New Adam. I suspect that it should be, and I also suspect that it exposes the most serious perplexities surrounding that doctrine—and perhaps resolves them as well.

Modern study has turned up a number of findings, none of which, perhaps, is sufficient by itself to validate reading the passage as a statement about Jesus in his humanity, but which cumulatively make a very strong case for it. Most important, perhaps, is a remarkably similar passage in Plutarch (*De Alexandri fortuna aut virtute*, 1, 8, fin.), in which it is stated that Alexander did not overrun Asia like a brigand, or treat it as booty (*harpagma*), but, wishing to make all mankind a single people, subjects of one Logos, he "fashioned himself" (*eschēmatisen*) like the local populace, assuming their dress when he came among them. Plutarch is writing almost a century later than Paul, of course; but since it is unlikely that he would be influenced by Paul, it must be that both the passage in Plutarch and the Christian hymn are making use of the same tradition of imagery. The most likely source is the Stoics and Cynics, who in their exhortations to a life of moral integrity and steadfastness took as their standard example Heracles, the son of Zeus, who in obedience to his divine father debased himself and endured many hardships, and consequently was accounted worthy to become the thirteenth god in the pantheon.[17] Ehrhardt, whose Chris-

---

17. See especially Arnold A. T. Ehrhardt, "Jesus Christ and Alexander the Great," *Journal of Theological Studies*, XLVI (1945): 45–51, reprinted in *The Framework of the New Testament Stories* (Manchester: Manchester University Press, and Cambridge, Mass.: Harvard University Press, 1964), pp. 37–43, and translated as "Ein antikes Herrscherideal: Phil. 2, 5–11," *Evangelische Theologie*, VIII (1948-49): 101–10. W. L. Knox, "The 'Divine Hero' Christology in the New Testament," *Harvard Theological Review*, XLI (1948): 229–49, deals more broadly with this motif in the New Testament and its parallels in the Hellenistic religious and philosophical world. Dieter Georgi, "Der vorpaulinische Hymnus Phil. 2, 6–11," *Zeit und Geschichte. Dankesgabe an Rudolf Bultmann zum 80. Geburtstag*, ed. Erich Dinkler (Tübingen: J. C. B. Mohr, 1964), pp. 263–93, also notes the many parallels between the hymn and the Hellenistic Jewish work *The Wisdom of Solomon* (itself influenced by Stoicism), especially chaps. 5 and 18, which depict the righteous man and his enemies.

tian commitments brought him into conflict with the rulers of his native Germany, adds with some animus that the hymn is not a mere pious utterance but a statement of the alternatives of thievery and service before which every authority, indeed every private person, stands, and that it puts Christ in the place of not only the demigods but the deified emperors of antiquity.

Even if this is the motif (as I think it is) not all problems are thereby solved. What is it that Christ gave up by emptying himself? What is the "equality with God" (or rather the "being as God," since it is an adverbial phrase, *einai isa theōi*) that he refused to count as "booty"? This has been a well-known *crux interpretum* since the seventeeth century, for "booty" (*harpagmos*) could mean either something already possessed (*res rapta*) or something which one is trying to possess (*res rapienda*); in addition, the same word was used in a metaphorical way to refer to a lucky find, a windfall, an opportunity, which, once more, could be either already possessed or still to be possessed.[18] But even when the exact force of the term—or rather the whole idiomatic expression—is puzzled out, it still does not help greatly toward construing the passage as a whole. If the divine mode of existence should be something already possessed, it could mean, of course, that the agent described here is a preexistent divine being, perhaps the Logos himself. But it could also mean that he is a human being of special stature, a *theios anēr*, since *isotheos* was a common epithet in the Greek world for heroes and religious geniuses; or perhaps that he fills a role like that of the archetypal man in the *Poimandres* (*Corpus Hermeticum*, I, 12), who is also called equal to the divine Nous (*autōi ison*). If, on the other hand, the divine mode of being is something still sought after, it could mean that the man Jesus is contrasted with the devil, who wished to be lord over the world; or with Adam and Eve, who tried to become "like God" (Gen. 3:5 and 22, LXX). But it could

18. The idiomatic use was pointed out in a classic article by Werner Jaeger, "Eine stilgeschichtliche Studie zum Philipperbrief," *Hermes*, L (1915): 537–53 and since that time there has been further debate over its exact import. The most careful and convincing study thus far is Roy W. Hoover, "The Harpagmos Enigma: A Philological Solution," *Harvard Theological Review*, LXIV (1971): 95–119, which concedes that the term can be used in the sense of a windfall, as it often was, but notes that the Philippians passage, like parallel passages in later Greek literature, is characterized by the *double accusative*, and in this construction it regularly connotes "counting the occasion as something to seize upon or take advantage of." *Harpagmos* refers, therefore, to the mental attitude of seizing the occasion for one's own advantage.

also mean that a preexistent angelic being, of less than divine rank, resisted the temptation to make himself godlike and as a reward for his humility was in the end exalted above his original state and given the name above all other names.

Each of these readings of the passage has been defended by critical scholars with a multitude of good reasons. My own preference would be to make the passage refer to the human Jesus and contrast him in some way with Adam. If the provenance of the hymn should be somewhere in the Hellenistic thought-world (and of course this would include Hellenistic Judaism of the sort reflected in Philo and the *Poimandres*), it would not be surprising to find a divine mode of being ascribed to Jesus, as either a man united with God or, somewhat more mythically, a figure similar to the primal man, still inhabiting the divine realm. Within Palestinian Judaism (or at least a strictly orthodox Palestinian Judaism) such ideas would not be so common, and we might anticipate a contrast between Jesus' humility and Adam's pride. Certainly this was a major part of Paul's thinking in other passages. But without excluding altogether the overtones suggesting this latter comparison, the overwhelming evidence is on the side of the other reading of the passage. Its language is so strongly influenced by Hellenistic religious currents that we must probably interpret it in their light and understand this mode of being "as God" as a state in which Jesus already existed and which he refused to exploit for his own advantage. (Adam, by contrast, would *not* be already existing "as God" in the same sense, and this would be something that he tried, improperly, to grasp at. Thus we would not rule out a comparison with the Adam of Genesis 2–3 but we must exclude the "adoptionist" line of thought that might be implied by the "two Adams" motif—as though Adam and Christ were in the same initial situation, and the difference in outcome is made by the disobedience of the one and the obedience of the other.)

It is impossible to say conclusively whether the self-emptying of Jesus takes place after his birth and growth in the flesh, or whether some kind of preexistence is assumed. There were enough mythic notions in circulation to make it entirely possible that preexistence could be involved; but it is worth pointing out that the very act of applying a mythic image—preexistence, archetypal man, Heracles, or whatever—to an earthly, historical figure like Jesus effects a kind of demythologization, bringing the image out of the ideal realm of myth, where it had been placed because of its contrast with actual human life, into the familiar realm of human decision and interaction.[19]

If the preponderance of evidence is on the side of those who stress the background in Hellenistic myth, then the passage will not be among those characteristic Pauline depictions of Jesus as the New Adam who, in a situation similar to that of the old Adam, reenacts the decisions by which the first Adam fell and thereby renews human life. It starts at a point farther back and more mysterious—signaled in those other passages by the expression *image of God*—from which all of that takes its rise. In this passage it is assumed that at the beginning Jesus is already in a situation of unity with God (however it is conceived, and however it might have arisen), and all the interest is directed toward his voluntarily sharing the lot of fallen mankind, much in the fashion of pagan redeemers like Heracles or Asclepius, or Plato's wise man who reenters the cave in which his fellow men are still imprisoned. The contrast between the "form of God" and the "form of a slave" does not necessarily imply a difference of natures, as though prior to his self-emptying he was not human but divine; the term *form* (*morphē*) is probably not used here in its technical Aristotelian sense

---

19. This is the opportune place, I think, for a discussion of the vexed problem of the origins of the early Christologies involving preexistence and the Logos, and their possible relation to "mythic" thinking. With all necessary deference to the detailed findings of historical study in this complex and uncertain field, I will confess my own suspicions that the thought processes of the early Christians ran somewhat as follows: first a sense of the unique status of Jesus, as expressed in titles like Messiah and Lord; then a systematic contrast between Jesus and other men, expressed in titles like Son of Man and Second Adam, which already involved, as we have seen, some notion of preexistence; and finally a reflection on the mode of this preexistence, sometimes pausing at the Gnostic view that primal humanity is in some sense divine, sometimes going on to the fully Platonist conclusion that it must be an idea in the divine Logos, or the divine Logos focused purposefully upon an outcome in the finite world. Paul's own thinking is still rather indistinct. The completion of this "trajectory" is to be found in the Letter to the Hebrews, where Jesus is identified with the divine Logos but with the paradoxical effect that, rather than being linked with creation and the primal nature of man, he is held in reserve until the time of fulfillment, as the model to which the Aaronic priesthood has been only an imperfect witness. There is, in other words, a heightening of the tension between the actuality and the ideal until the ideal "appears," once and for all, at the end of the age (Heb. 9:26). It is not surprising, then, to find that notions like man's dominion over the earth, or God's rest at the end of the six days of creation, are snatched away from the beginning of things and are declared to be unrealized at any point short of the resurrection of Jesus and his saints (Heb. 2:5–9 and 4:3–11; cf. the Epistle of Barnabas, 6:19 and 15:6–7). The mythic "primal world" is transformed into a Platonist "world of ideas," where it gains critical relevance through contrast with present reality and exerts pressure toward future transformations.

of nature or essence, but in a more casual way, as having to do with a mode of existence or a style of life.[20] The passage would mean, then, that Jesus, even though he was and remained in the form of God—in a divine mode of being, probably equivalent with "image of God"—freely entered into the human condition, in complete likeness to other men, sharing their situation but without sin (cf. Rom. 8:3). The stress is upon this redemptive intention toward others; this is what establishes the connection between Jesus and enslaved humanity. It is only then, after describing Jesus' sharing of the human condition, that Paul, or the pre-Pauline hymnodist, comes, in the third strophe, to the motif of obedience which is generally more characteristic of Paul's New Adam doctrine.

What all of this means is that the obedience of Jesus in contrast to Adam's disobedience, and thus his function as Second Adam in relation to others, does not constitute, for Paul, the central mystery in Jesus' person; prior to his relation to the others there is his relation to God. On the other hand, he does not simply remain within this private relationship with God but shares the human condition; his renewal of human life is accomplished not through what he is within himself, as a kind of example or holy object, but through just this participation in the general human condition. The primary emphasis, to be sure, falls upon what is inward; but it is an inwardness that opens out toward others, not shunning them as a threat to his own precious subjectivity. Therefore Paul can urge upon his readers, in the immediate context (Phil. 2:1–4; cf. Rom. 15:3 and 2 Cor. 8:9) the same kind of self-abandoned concern for the needs of others, the same kind of acceptance of the mutability, vulnerability, and mortality of human life. The same verb of attitude or evaluation (*hēgesthai*) which is used in the expression *he did not count it booty* is employed repeatedly in the next chapter in connection with Paul's own attitude toward his status as a Jew, a Pharisee, a man blameless before the Law (Phil. 3:7–11):

> But whatever gain I had, I counted as loss for the sake of Christ. Indeed, I count everything as loss because of the surpassing worth of knowing Christ Jesus my Lord. For his sake I have suffered the loss of all things, and count them as refuse in order that I may gain Christ and be found in him, not having a righteousness of my own, based on law,

20. Cf., among other discussions, Käsemann, *Exegetische Versuche und Besinnungen*, I: 67–68.

but that which is through faith in Christ, the righteousness from God
that depends on faith; that I may know him and the power of his resurrection, and may share his sufferings, becoming like him in his death,
that if possible I may attain the resurrection from the dead.

The relationship between Jesus and the others is in the last analysis
established and cemented by personal attitudes and purposes and commitments from both sides, asymmetrical, to be sure, but mutual nonetheless. Despite the radical differences between the initiative taken by
Christ, in union with God and in keeping with God's purposes, and the
fundamentally uncreative and therefore dependent and receptive role
of those who have been accosted by him, there is still a likeness in that
both are led to accept the human situation and live on terms of co-hu-
manity with all their brothers and sisters.

This survey of the key passages in Paul's writings confirms, I think,
the view that the significance of Jesus lies principally in his renewed
humanity, that the "mediator between God and man" is, according to a
deutero-Pauline phrase that the Church fathers liked to quote, "the
man Christ Jesus" (1 Tim. 2:5). But it is not an easy matter, as we
have seen, to explain just how Jesus does have relevance to others, or
even to say in what sense he is the renewed man.

We have encountered, first of all, the simple and absolute characterization of Jesus as the New Adam or the image of God. This even by
itself is important because it establishes his community of nature—and
of task—with all men and at the same time his unique function in relation to them. But then a tension is introduced by the general alienation
of men from God, and as a consequence even this characterization as
the New Adam acquires a certain complexity. At the very least, it is
made in terms of a contrast between Adam and Christ. But we find
that Paul also insists upon a contrast between Christ and believers,
who must be related to him not simply through direct imitation or
mystical participation, but through the gospel of the cross and resurrection (2 Cor. 4:3–4). The pre-Pauline hymn in Philippians 2, furthermore, even attempts to get "inside" Christ and speaks of his condescension to share the general human condition, his willingness to serve
others rather than please himself or take advantage of his status for his
own benefit. There is even a suggestion—developed much further in
the Epistle to the Hebrews—of an element of human struggle and
temptation along the way to his exaltation.

All of these are complications introduced by the tension between sin and redemption. But there is one more element of instability and incompleteness that is, in a sense, even more fundamental than the struggle with sin. Certainly it is more ultimate. This is the eschatological dimension, which perhaps will not seem to be a part of the motif of the image of God (associated as the latter is with the beginnings of the human race) until we recognize that the image of God involves a *task*, not a finished and guaranteed *state*. Certainly this is true of Adam, who seems to be given the title only grudgingly and with reservations; but it is true even of Christ, whose significance for others is not restricted to his earthly life and death but extends to his resurrection, and whose work is not finished until all his brothers and sisters "bear the image of the man of heaven" (1 Cor. 15:49) and "he delivers the kingdom to God the Father" (1 Cor. 15:24). Thus it is not enough to link him with Adam or the Primal Man, or to make him the decisive turning point of human history as the New Adam. The only resting point, the focus upon which all the lines of force converge, is the eschaton itself, in which fulfillment is at last attainable under altogether different conditions.

With a scope as vast as this, it is not surprising that Paul's thought could be interpreted in varying ways and evoke a number of different problems, chief among which, for our purposes, is the place of Christ in the divine plan as a whole.

The Pauline theme of the first and second Adam was carried forward and elaborated in a classic way by Irenaeus in books III-V of his work against the heresies of his day, entitled *Exposure and Overturning of What Is Falsely Called Knowledge,* and incidentally in the *Epideixis* or *Exhibition of the Apostolic Message.*[21] But Irenaeus is not a sudden portent in the late second century, and we must note, as we go along, the points at which he seems to be leaning on earlier doctrinal traditions.

---

21. A suggestive though sometimes tendentious discussion of this aspect of Irenaeus will be found in Gustaf Wingren, *Man and the Incarnation: A Study in the Biblical Theology of Irenaeus,* trans. Ross Mackenzie (Philadelphia: Muhlenberg Press, 1959). See also Martin Widmann, "Irenäus und seine theologischen Väter," *Zeitschrift für Theologie und Kirche,* LIV (1957): 156–73, and André Benoit, *Saint Irénée. Introduction à l'étude de sa théologie* (Etudes d'histoire et de philosophie religieuses, LII; Paris: Presses Universitaires de France, 1960). In citations from book III of Irenaeus' work, I follow the chapter numberings of Massuet and the Patrologia, which differ from Harvey's.

In Irenaeus' work there are two ways in which Adam and Christ are related to each other. The stress is sometimes upon *continuity*, so that Christ is the completion of a development that began (or rather should have begun) with Adam; sometimes upon the *opposition* between Adam's disobedience and Christ's righteousness. It seems likely that the antitheses, elaborated in great detail, between Adam and Christ, Eve and Mary, the tree of knowledge and the tree of the crucifixion, the serpent as first victorious and then conquered, are drawn from the writings of Justin Martyr, set down in Rome between 150 and 165.[22] This is striking because Justin himself made no use of the Pauline epistles as authoritative Christian writings. Apparently they were not yet recognized by the Church in Rome, and even worse, they were in the hands of the Marcionites, who used them to draw a sharp contrast between the Old Testament and the New, between the Creator with his retributive justice and the Hidden God who in mercy rescues men. It is still possible that Justin's antitheses between Adam and Christ owe something to Paul; but it would have to be indirectly, through the Marcionites. If so, he has reconverted the Marcionites' views into something more akin to Paul's own thought. Of course there could have been other lines of tradition, stemming from Paul or from a common Christian teaching, comparing Christ with Adam. But what characterizes Justin's thought, and sets it apart from Paul and his authentic successors, is a radical sharpening of the opposition between Adam and Christ. Not only is there an antithesis in all their acts; there is not even a continuity between them, for Justin insists that Christ is in every sense a "new creation," born "through Mary" but not "from Mary," coming into being not out of a human lineage but created directly from unformed matter, perhaps with a divine ichor flowing in his veins.[23]

Irenaeus does not follow Justin here. Where Justin said that Jesus was born "through the virgin," Irenaeus says that he was born "from the virgin" and stresses the continuity between Adam and Christ, the

---

22. The chief passages in Irenaeus are *Adv. haer.*, III, 21, 10; 22, 3–4; 23, 1; IV, 20, 8; V, 16, 3; 17, 3–4; 19, 1; and *Epideixis*, 30–37; in Justin, *Dialogue with Trypho*, 45, 94, 100, 103.

23. *Dial.*, 54, 63, 76; *Apol. I*, 32; cf. Celsus' mocking remarks in Origen, *Contra Celsum*, I, 66 and II, 36. The parallel was pointed out by Henry Chadwick in *Early Christian Thought and the Classical Tradition* (Oxford: Oxford University Press, 1966), p. 133.

latter inheriting the very same nature that was handed on from the former. The parallel between Adam and Christ cannot be, therefore, that both are formed *de novo* from unformed matter, as Justin thought; it must be that both are formed directly by God (this is the explicit argument of III, 21, 9–22, 2).[24] Irenaeus thus sees a basic continuity between Christ and the history of the human race, both before and after him, and it is well known that he repeatedly speaks in this connection of *anakephalaiōsis* (*recapitulatio*), and thinks of recapitulation as the execution, in history, of a divine plan or *oikonomia* (*dispensatio*).[25]

This term *anakephalaiōsis* can have several distinct meanings, and they are all to be found in Irenaeus' own work.[26] When it is used with reference to rhetorical or literary practice, it can mean, first of all, a returning to something previously mentioned (I, 9, 2) or a starting over again from the beginning, a repeating or reiterating of something said earlier (V, 33, 4). This meaning of recapitulation would be quite compatible with Justin's theme that there is a similarity of function between Adam and Christ but an antithesis in the content of their acts. Irenaeus sometimes speaks of recapitulation in this sense. He says that Christ "effected a recapitulation of the disobedience at the tree, through obedience at the tree" (V, 19, 1); he also speaks of a "joining of the end to the beginning" in Luke's genealogy of Christ, which goes back to Adam, and a "circling back" from Mary to Eve when the bond

---

24. Albert Houssiau, *La Christologie de saint Irénée* (Louvain: Publications Universitaires, 1955), pp. 236–47.

25. Probably his authority for the use of both terms is Eph. 1:9–10, which speaks of "the mystery of [God's] will, according to his purpose which he set forth in Christ as an *oikonomia* for the fullness of time, to recapitulate all things in him, those in heaven and those on earth"; the passage was already being used by the Ptolemaeans, as Irenaeus' discussion in I, 3, 4 indicates. There is at least the possibility that Justin also used the term, for it is found in the continuation of a passage which Irenaeus expressly quotes from Justin's work against Marcion (*Adv. haer.*, IV, 11, 2); but the question is where the quotation from Justin stops, and it is more likely to be at just the point where Eusebius stopped while citing it in his *Ecclesiastical History* (IV, 18, 9), so that the mention of recapitulation is Irenaeus' own (James Armitage Robinson, "On a Quotation from Justin Martyr in Irenaeus," *Journal of Theological Studies*, XXXI [1930]: 374–78). Of course Justin *could* have used the term, but if he did its sense would be controlled by a very different understanding of the place of Christ in human history, as we have seen.

26. Cf. A. Scharl, "Der Rekapitulationsbegriff des heiligen Irenäus," *Orientalia Christiana Periodica*, VI (1940): 378; Albert Houssiau, *La Christologie de saint Irénée*, pp. 215–24 and 238–47; and Gregory T. Armstrong, *Die Genesis in der alten Kirche. Die drei Kirchenväter* (Beiträge zum Geschichte der biblischen Hermeneutik, IV; Tübingen: J. C. B. Mohr, 1962), pp. 61–67.

created by disobedience is dissolved and is replaced by another bond coming from obedience (III, 22, 3).

There is, however, a second and quite different meaning of the term in rhetoric and literature: a recapitulation is a summing up of the whole, giving a resumé, bringing to a head, as in IV, 2, 1, where Irenaeus says that in Deuteronomy Moses gave a summary or "recapitulation" of the law. This would seem closer to Irenaeus' usual understanding of the term.

But since the interpretation of Irenaeus' doctrine is so difficult, it seems best to look at his usage, not at the isolated term.

The agent or subject of the action is always the divine Word, sometimes preincarnate, sometimes incarnate. The act of recapitulating is not a simple one. It takes place through a whole succession of events which begin with the birth of Christ, his growth, temptation, death, and resurrection, and continue on through the history of the Church, concluding with the consummation.[27]

The object of the action is generally the humanity created in Adam and handed on from him, the *antiqua plasmatio*. There seems to be a systematic correlation, in fact, between the act of "molding" Adam and the recapitulation of this same *plasmatio* in Christ (III, 21, 10–22, 1). In one passage, to be sure, there is a stress upon "all things," as in Eph. 1:10. But even then the focus remains anthropological, for the point is that

> the invisible becomes visible, the incomprehensible becomes comprehensible, the impassible becomes passible, the Word becomes man, in order that the Word of God, who is already ruler among the things that are above the heavens and spiritual and invisible, might also have rule among visible and corporeal things, taking the primacy upon himself and making himself head of the Church, drawing all things to himself at the appropriate time. (III, 16, 6)

The goal or *terminus* of the action, although it is usually overlooked, is the most revealing feature of Irenaeus' thought, for he always says that it is the Word himself. The usual expression is that the Word recapitulates the old *plasmatio* "toward himself" or "into himself" (*"recapitulans in seipsum," "anakephalaiōsamenos eis auton"*—the Greek is preserved in III, 22, 2 and IV, 38, 1).

27. See especially Wingren, *Man and the Incarnation*, pp. 79–90.

Houssiau is probably correct, then, in suggesting that the meaning of the term *recapitulation* is to be gained not from rhetorical usage but from the connotations suggested by its etymology. Recapitulation would be, then, a bringing up or back toward the head, a *"ramener à son principe,"* that is to say, a leading of man, who was once molded by the Logos, back into unity with the Logos.[28] As Irenaeus works out this recapitulation theme, Adam and Eve were created in the condition of a child (*nēpios, infans* [IV, 38, 1; cf. Epideixis, 46 and 96]), by which he means not only that they were innocent, lacking experience and discernment, but that they were literally children, naked but still unaware of their sexuality, preadolescent (III, 22, 3). They stood only at the beginning of what was to have been a long process of development, and of course that development has been distorted by sin and is resumed and restored in Christ.

> When the Word was incarnate and became man, he recapitulated the long story of mankind in himself, offering salvation to us all at once, summed up [*in compendio, syntomōs*], so that what we lost in Adam—namely, to be according to the image and likeness of God—we might receive in Christ Jesus. (III, 18, 1)

Because there was to have been this long process of development, what is offered in Christ is more than Adam ever possessed:

> In earlier times it was only *said* that man was made according to the image of God, but it was not *shown*, for the Word according to whose image man was made remained unseen. Because of this he easily lost his likeness to God. But when the Word of God was made flesh, he confirmed both assertions: he showed forth the true image by himself becoming that which had arisen as the image of himself, and he confirmed the likeness by restoring it, making man similar to the invisible Father through the visible Word. (V, 16, 1)

It is not surprising, in view of this developmental conception of the history of the race even under the best of conditions, that Irenaeus interprets Paul's "two Adams" doctrine to mean that God predestined the first man to be merely "animate" in order that he might be saved by the "spiritual" man (III, 22, 3). This does not mean that sin itself was

---

28. Houssiau, *La Christologie de saint Irénée*, pp. 218, 227.

decreed by God; rather it indicates that Irenaeus is a "Christocentrist" who views the incarnation as the culmination of human development, a culmination which would be indispensable even apart from sin, since it is only through it that they should properly be brought from innocence to full knowledge (cf. *Epideixis*, 12).

It is apparent that this motif of gradual development is altogether different from what Irenaeus would have acquired from Justin. But Friedrich Loofs noted its similarity to the ideas expressed by Theophilus of Antioch in his one surviving work, the apology addressed to Autolycus, and suggested that Irenaeus might have been utilizing a larger work by Theophilus against Marcion, mentioned by Eusebius but now lost.[29] Like Theophilus, Irenaeus often calls the Word and the Spirit the two "hands" of God, and the *plasmatio* theme in Irenaeus is reminiscent of Theophilus' statement (*Ad Autol.*, II, 18) that man is the only creature God deemed worthy of being made with his own hands and not merely called into being. Furthermore, the extensive discussion of the situation of Adam in Theophilus (II, 24–27) has many points of correspondence with Irenaeus. He says that God made man from earth and then set him in Paradise, midway between heaven and earth, to show that he was neither definitively mortal nor definitively immortal but was capable of becoming either, according to the use he made of his free choice (cf. Iren., *Adv. haer.*, V, 9–13); the tree of knowledge was not entirely forbidden to man, being promised to him after he matured, but in the meantime he was to remain simple and obedient, as a child to a parent, and await the time when he could use knowledge suitably (cf. Iren., *Adv. haer.*, IV, 38; V, 23). The similarities are so striking that Loofs's hypothesis is more convincing than the attempts to refute it.

Although this makes Irenaeus less original than he first appears, his own contribution is still an impressive one, for he seems to have brought together the motif of continuity and development from Theophilus and that of opposition from Justin, combining them within a theological framework unified by the divine "economy" directed

29. Friedrich Loofs, *Theophilus von Antiochien adversus Marcionem und die anderen theologischen Quellen bei Irenaeus* (Texte und Untersuchungen, XLVI, 2; Leipzig: J. C. Hinrichs, 1930). Loofs's thesis, although it is obviously problematical and has frequently been attacked, has also been viewed with favor by many subsequent scholars (e.g., Widmann and Benoit, previously cited).

toward the recapitulation of humanity and of human development in Christ.[30] Whatever he may have learned from others, and however imperfectly he may have drawn it all together, he genuinely deserves to have his name linked with one of the most durable interpretations of the Pauline theme of the New Adam, one that has the merit of taking seriously the difference between beginning and fulfillment and thus of giving a place to the slow growth and gradual improvement that are such an obvious feature of human history. Irenaeus was, to be sure, a Christocentrist, believing that the human race must remain in tutelage, even apart from sin, until the Logos should come to instruct men face to face. The chief reasons for his position are his sense that gradual growth is the law of human life and his healthy appreciation of the contrast between the humanity that existed at the beginning and the humanity that could come into being. Neither of these necessarily implies an incarnation of the ideal in a sinless world, and in fact the influence of Irenaeus in the patristic period did *not* include this feature, for reasons that should become clear as we look at the themes that especially occupied its writers.

2. The Omnipresence of the Logos

One of the strongest motives for a thoroughgoing Christocentrism is the notion that God is basically unknown to humanity until he makes himself personally present to them in the incarnation. This could be said with varying degrees of seriousness. It was asserted quite literally by the Marcionites and the Valentinians and other gnosticizing groups within the early Church who thought that God was totally hidden from man until the descent of the Redeemer. But there are tendencies in this direction even in "safe" writings, the Pauline corpus and the Fourth Gospel and the letters of Ignatius, where it is assumed that man is enslaved to the sensible world and the cosmic powers, not because of some cosmic tragedy (as in the Gnostics) but because of sin. These writers would all be ready to acknowledge that God has made himself known in the Scriptures inherited from Israel, and even that he can be known through the cosmos. But they sometimes seem to imply that Christ gives a knowledge of God that is new not only in degree but in kind, and then there is a danger (actualized among the Marcionites,

---

30. This is the argument running throughout the Widmann article cited above.

who used Paul, and the Valentinians, who used the Fourth Gospel)
that their thought will slip into radical Gnostic patterns.

It was in reaction against the Gnostic sects and their interpretations
of the New Testament writings that the first self-conscious "theologians" of the Church—Justin, Theophilus, Irenaeus, Tertullian, Clement,
Origen—elaborated, with the aid of Greek philosophy and the authori-
zation and encouragement of the biblical tradition, the doctrine of the
Logos.[31] They saw the Logos as the principle by which God is related
to the world, both as the formative influence in creation and providence, and as the source of whatever rationality and wisdom man
attains. Justin Martyr and Clement of Alexandria in particular are
noted for the generosity with which they credit many of the great men
of the Greek past (Socrates, certainly, but also Heraclitus and others)
with an awareness of the Logos and a responsiveness to its promptings
(Justin, *Apol.* I, 46; Clement, *Strom.*, II, 43–44; V, 133–134; VI, 44 ff.).
This is possible because in each person a "seed" of the Logos is
implanted (*Apol.* II, 8), or each person has a "part" in the Logos (*Apol.*
II, 10); what is then needed is to let this develop, with the aid of
grace, into a full participation and imitation of the Logos (*Apol.* II,
13). The context of all this is the assumption, common to nearly all
schools of philosophy in antiquity, that man's true rationality is quite
directly dependent upon a factor beyond himself, often conceived to
be a mind superior to man (Plato, Aristotle, the Stoics), and, beyond
this epistemological assumption, their belief that man's proper destiny
lay in living according to reason and coming into more intimate contact with the ground of rationality.

Although subsequent theologians were not so quick to ascribe to
pagan philosophers an intimate communion with the Logos and call
them "Christians," as Justin did (*Apol.* I, 46), the Logos theology remained nonetheless a standard element of patristic thought. Even those
who hesitated to impute salvation to any Gentiles who had not had
contact with the biblical tradition still made use of the Logos doctrine
in their depiction of the original situation of man and the life that the

31. Discussions of this theme are numerous, of course, but among those in English
I would single out both one of the first, Edwin Hatch's 1888 Hibbert Lectures,
The Influence of Greek Ideas and Usages upon the Christian Church (London:
Williams & Norgate, 1890; reprinted Harper Torchbooks, 1957), lecture VII, and
one of the most recent, Henry Chadwick's *Early Christian Thought and the
Classical Tradition* (Oxford: Oxford University Press, 1966).

human race might have enjoyed had Adam not sinned; for they regularly described the primitive state as one of communion with the divine Logos, made possible by the Spirit's giving purity and transparency to the human mind. This was lost, however, with man's sin, so that his mind was darkened and his will became unstable, and only then was it necessary for him to be given revelation through sensible media.

Perhaps the chief hurdle for people unacquainted with the framework of patristic thought (which is quite different from the understanding of God and incarnation that has somehow been handed on in ordinary Christian instruction, by "convention" as distinguished from "tradition") is that incarnation is *not* thought to be indispensable if God is to enter into relation with the world, or to love persons, even to sympathize with them. Nor is it the only means by which God can redeem men, for the fathers discerned in the whole history of salvation, from the "protoevangelium" (Gen. 3:15) and Abel onward, the work of the divine Logos. They had a confidence, based upon their acquaintance with Platonist and Stoic philosophy and the late biblical passages influenced by it, that persons are set in relation to the *unincarnate* Logos. (I have in mind passages like Wisdom 7, Hebrews 1, Colossians 1, and John 1, which, whatever the scholars may finally discover about their intervening career in the history of religious syncretism and early Christian tradition, still bear the traces of their philosophical ancestry and were interpreted in a philosophical way by the fathers.)

It would be a mistake to suppose that this general relevance of the Logos to the world and to human life was understood in a way somehow extraneous to Christian concern. (At this point Karl Barth, sorely tempted by historians like Ritschl and Harnack and Loofs, repeatedly sins against historical honesty, perversely insisting that any Logos outside the incarnation is alien to Christian faith.)[32] On the contrary, it enabled Christian thinkers to take all aspects of nature and human life seriously, at their face value (that is, not sneaking hidden religious values into them), and still have the confidence that the whole wealth of experience is drawn together and unified when man finds his proper relation to the divine Word and gains true wisdom and righteousness. To them the incarnation is, of course, the chief manifestation of the Logos, unique and unparalleled. Still it is one among many manifesta-

32. See especially *CD*, III/2, 130–32; IV/1, 52; and IV/2, 33–34.

tions, and not entirely unlike the others. Perhaps one must speak of an analogy between this and other manifestations, involving both similarities (enabling one to apply the same interpretative scheme, the same metaphysical coordinates, to all of them) and differences (requiring the coordinates to be "bent," so to speak, in a non-Euclidean way). It is sometimes said that the fathers thought in terms of an "incarnational universe," and this is correct, I suppose, as long as it is made clear that they did not see all else as a sub-case of the incarnation but viewed the incarnation as one instance of a more general relationship of the Logos to that which is not God.

One of the chief causes of resistance to this classic view, I am sure, is an objection arising from religious sensibility, a suspicion that it envisages an abrupt change in God's plans, so that he is first in heaven and then enters the world. But such an objection, although it would apply to ancient Gnosticism, which imagined a sudden and unique plunge into the world, does not apply to the anti-Gnostic thought of the fathers, who understood God to be intimately involved with the cosmos and history throughout and did not suppose this to be necessarily bound up with a decision to become incarnate.

Indeed, the fathers had a positive reason for *not* being drawn into a thoroughgoing Christocentrism. In the last analysis it seems to be (and this may surprise those with preconceptions about the thought-world of the fathers) a sense of the dramatic character of human history, as suggested by the biblical account of sin and salvation. This was not even counteracted by their Platonist leanings, for we must remember that in the ancient world Platonism meant, before all else, the Orphic doctrine of the soul's journeys and the cosmology of the *Timaeus*. While it is true that both features of Platonism were often interpreted unhistorically, in terms of eternal recurrence (by Aristotle, and by middle Platonists of the so-called school of Gaius, and by Plotinus and neo-Platonism), there was a rival historical interpretation, associated with Atticus and Plutarch, and it is this brand of Platonism that was followed by philosophically conscious writers like Justin and Origen and Eusebius.[33] To be sure, some Christian thinkers understood the

33. See especially Hal Koch, *Pronoia und Paideusis. Studien über Origenes und sein Verhältnis zum Platonismus* (Berlin and Leipzig: Walter de Gruyter, 1932), pp. 237–43; Carl Andresen, "Justin und der mittlere Platonismus," *Zeitschrift für die neutestamentliche Wissenschaft*, XLIV (1953): 157–95; Henry Chadwick, *Early Christian Thought and the Classical Tradition*, pp. 108–11.

drama as a strangely disembodied one at its beginning (I have in mind Origen and his many admirers), but even they saw it, quite unmistakably, as a drama. Since this is the core of their position, the reason that they insisted so strongly that the function of the incarnation was redemptive and that it would not have occurred apart from sin, we should examine their discussions in some detail.

3. The Incarnation in God's Purposes

The tone of the patristic discussion of the incarnation is set by Origen, with his vivid sense of dramatic interplay between creaturely freedom and divine justice. In his commentary on John (*PG*, XIV, 57–60; *GCS*, X, 25), while taking note of the immense number of titles given to Christ in the Scriptures, he observes that most of them refer to contingent relationships:

> Supposing that the woman had not been deceived, and Adam had not fallen, and man created for incorruption had attained it, then he would not have descended to mortal dust, nor would he have died, there being no sin; nor would his love for men have required that he die, and if he had not died, he would not have been the first-born of the dead. It should also be asked whether he would ever have become a shepherd, had man not descended to the level of the beasts which are devoid of reason and become like them. . . . Thus it is appropriate to collect the titles of the Son and ask which of them were conferred on him later and would never have existed if the holy ones had begun and persevered in blessedness. . . . And happy indeed are those who in their need for the Son of God have become such as not to need him as a physician healing the sick, or as a shepherd, or as redemption, but only as Wisdom and Word and Righteousness, or any other title suitable for those who, because of their perfection, are able to receive that which is fairest about him.

Other writers took the same view. In most instances they merely let their assumptions be expressed in by-the-way remarks; but there are a few explicit discussions which show that the shared assumptions of that period could stand in the face of further reflection.

The whole second half of Athanasius' second oration against the Arians (*Or.* II *c. Ar.*, 44–82) is a discussion of the difficult passage in Prov. 8:22 in which Wisdom says (according to the Septuagint, of course), "The Lord created me as the beginning of his ways, for his works" (*Kyrios ektisen me archēn hodōn autou eis erga autou*). Unlike some other interpreters, Athanasius refuses to explain away the term *created*. The passage means what it says, and if he is to avoid the Arian heresy (the view that the Word is created and thus is not of the same nature as God) he must say that Wisdom, the divine Word, is speaking not in its eternal being but in its relation to the created realm. Actually he finds two interpretations of the statement. One of them links it to his remarkable theory of creation through condescension (*Or.* II *c. Ar.*, 63–64; 78–82): the Word gives being, and makes all things good, by accommodating himself to the capacities of the finite and uniting himself with it, much in the manner of the Platonist World-Soul, so that all things cohere in him; thus he can be called the "first-born of all creation" (cf. Col. 1:15–17) and can speak, in their behalf, of being "created for his works" (Prov. 8:22). The other interpretation links it to the incarnation, and specifically to the act in which, from eternity, the incarnation is decided upon. This act takes place as "the beginning of his ways," with a view toward the economy of salvation. And if Wisdom is "created," it is created *for* these works:

> If it is not for himself but for us that he has come, it is not for himself but *for us* that he is created; and if he is created not for himself but for us, then he is not himself a creature; but he uses such language *as having put on our flesh.* (*Or.* II *c. Ar.*, 55, italics added).

This "being created" before the beginning of the earth is nothing else, then, than the predestination of Christ and of the elect in him, the preparation of a kingdom before the foundation of the world—in sum, the planning out of the whole economy of salvation (*Or.* II, 75–77).

This line of thought, which seems to lead in the direction of a Christocentrist view of creation (so that the passage has often been cited as the patristic *locus classicus* for that view), is used with precisely the opposite force. Even at the beginning, Athanasius says, God was not ignorant of human destiny; he foresaw man's transgression and "prepared beforehand in his own Word, by whom he created us, the economy of our salvation" (*Or.* II, 75). As a wise architect thinks about repairs even before he begins building a house, God in his goodness and wisdom prepares a remedy for sin even before creating man (*Or.* II, 77); and it is clear that the remedy is prepared only because of the actual fall of man, foreknown by God:

Man's need preceded [the Word's] becoming man, and apart from it he would not have put on flesh. (*Or.* II, 54)

His becoming man would not have taken place had not the need of men become a "cause" of God's acting. (*Or.* II, 56)

The same doctrine is expressed in the striking notion of *felix culpa*, formulated by Ambrose in a number of his sermons—that the fall of man, rebellious and ruinous as it is, has been more fruitful and beneficial to man in the long run than was the state of innocence, since it occasioned all the benefits of redeeming grace, causing God to manifest his goodness in a supreme way and confer upon man a higher mode of life than he would have enjoyed if Adam had not sinned. It was given an abiding place in the spirituality of the Church with the *Exultet* hymn of the Holy Saturday liturgy, perhaps written by Ambrose himself: "*O felix culpa quae talem ac tantum meruit habere redemptorem.*"[34] It is also to be found, in somewhat more magisterial rhythms, in the so-called Tome of Pope Leo, sent to the Council of Chalcedon:

Since the devil was glorying in the fact that man, deceived by his craft, was bereft of divine gifts and, being stripped of this endowment of immortality, had come under the harsh sentence of death, and that he himself, amid his miseries, had found consolation in having a transgressor as his companion, and that God, in keeping with the requirements of justice, had changed his own judgment concerning man, whom he had created in such a high position of honor, there was need of a dispensation of secret counsel, in order that the unchangeable God, whose will could not be deprived of its own generosity, should fulfill by a more secret mystery his original plan of loving kindness toward us, and that man, who had been led into fault by the wicked subtlety of the devil, should not perish contrary to God's purpose. (3, fin.)

We should note that the incarnation is not the only action of God that was considered to be contingent upon sin. Even more drastic is the view of many thinkers of this period that a part of God's creative activity is somehow the consequence of sin. The notion was expressed in several competing forms. Origen felt that the world itself, indeed, a whole succession of worlds, is created in order to put fallen souls in the

34. For this see Gerhart B. Ladner, *The Idea of Reform: Its Impact on Christian Thought and Action in the Age of the Fathers* (Cambridge, Mass.: Harvard University Press, 1959), pp. 146–47.

places suited to their moral condition and lead them gradually toward salvation. Gregory of Nyssa (*De opif. hom.*, 16–17 and 21–22) suggested that human beings were created with sexuality only because of God's foreknowledge that they would sin and lose their immortality, and that they acquired their earthly bodies (the "tunics of skin" of Gen. 3:21) after they actually committed sin. Augustine speculated toward the end of his career that the elect had been predestined to make up the number of the fallen angels (*De civ. Dei*, XXII, 1; *Enchir.*, 9, 29). Pope Gregory, following out this Augustinian line of speculation during a grimmer time, suggested that the human race was created only after the fall of the angels, and for the purpose of supplementing the nine depleted ranks of angels with a tenth group (*Hom. in evang.*, II, 34, 6–7 and 11 [*PL*, LXXVI, 1249–52]). By the time of Anselm (*Cur Deus homo?* I, 18) this isolated suggestion of Gregory's appears to have been taken up and asserted quite seriously.[35]

If the authoritative documents of the Church clearly taught that the work of Christ was related quite specifically to sinful man, how did the other opinion, that the incarnation would have had a place even apart from sin, come to arise?

It seems to be the outcome of meditation on the history of salvation and the counsel of God, meditation of the sort expressed in the title of Anselm's great work, *Cur Deus Homo?*, but not limited to him alone, since it is typical of the monastic milieu.[36] The immediate occasion was the asking of the contrary-to-fact question, "What *would have* happened, *if* Adam had *not* sinned?"

4. Incarnation without Fall?

This contrary-to-fact question was first raised by Rupert of Deutz about 1100. Although he did not answer it unequivocally, he pointed out that there would have been saints and elect even apart from sin and asked whether it might be necessary for the God-man to be their

---

35. The question was debated in the early twelfth century by Rupert of Deutz and Honorius of Autun, whom we shall meet again in connection with the rise of speculations about the reason for the incarnation (cf. M.-D. Chenu, "Cur homo? Le sous-sol d'une controverse," *La théologie au douzième siècle* [Etudes de philosophia médiévale, XLV; Paris; J. Vrin, 1957], pp. 52–61).

36. See Jean Leclercq, *The Love of Learning and the Desire for God: A Study of Monastic Culture*, trans. Catharine Misrahi (New York: Fordham University Press, 1961; Mentor-Omega Books, 1962).

Lord and King (*De gloria et honore Filii hominis* [*Comm. in Matt.*], XIII [*PL*, CLXVIII, 1628]). Again, he pointed out that God's intention was to make man "in his own image and likeness," but the narrative of the actual creation says only that he made man "in his image," as though to suggest that his creative purpose was not brought to fulfill-ment at the start, but is completed only in the incarnation of the Son and the outpouring of the Spirit (*De operibus Sp. Sanct.*, I, 11 [*PL*, CLXVII, 1580–82]).[37]

The first clear affirmation of the thesis is to be found in Honorius of Autun, writing about the same time:

> The sin of the first man was not the cause of Christ's incarnation; it was, if anything, the cause of man's death and condemnation. The cause of Christ's incarnation was, on the contrary, God's predestining man to deification, and Christ was predestined from eternity in order that man might be deified. . . . (*Libellus octo quaestionum de angelis et homine*, q. 2 [*PL*, CLXXII, 1187–88])

He takes marriage as a proof of this, for it is called a sacrament of Christ and the Church (Eph. 5:31–32) and it was in existence even before sin. His fundamental principle seems to be that God's counsel and predestination are immutable, and in any case they should not be altered by sin. He does acknowledge that sin makes a difference, for without it neither Christ nor anyone else would have died. But with a perfect sense for the appropriate resolution to this problem, he links Christ to the situation of men generally. From the perspective of the human situation prior to the fall, it is not yet determined whether Christ, like all men, will die or not, for this is contingent upon their sinning or not sinning. Once men sin, it becomes necessary for him, like them (but for a different reason), to die. But the incarnation brings with it the power to be tempted and not sin, and finally the res-

---

37. For a basic historical sketch of the development of Christocentrism, see Robert North, *Teilhard and the Creation of the Soul* (Saint Louis University Theology Studies, V; Milwaukee: Bruce, 1967), the fifth chapter of which, entitled "The Scotist Cosmic Christ," was delivered as a paper at the 1966 Scotus conference in Oxford (see pp. 119–62, and esp. pp. 139 ff.). Also helpful is Josef Bach, *Die Dogmengeschichte des Mittelalters vom christologischen Standpunkte, oder Die mittelalterliche Christologie vom achten bis sechzehnten Jahrhundert* (Vienna, 1875; reprinted Frankfurt: Minerva, 1966). Useful references can also be found in A. Michel, "Incarnation," *Dictionnaire de théologie catholique*, VII, 2 (Paris, 1927), esp. cols. 1495–1507, although its manner is more theological than histori-cal.

urrection of Christ makes death impossible, not only for him but for all those who link their destiny with his.

The Christocentrist position entered scholastic circles only slowly and with difficulty. In the so-called *Summa fratris Alexandri* (probably a joint enterprise of the Paris Franciscans under the direction of Alexander of Hales, with three books being completed before the deaths of Alexander and John of la Rochelle in 1245),[38] the new thesis is rejected in one of the earlier portions (II, inq. 1, tr. 2, q. 3, c. 6, a. 4) on the grounds that the incarnation would not have added to the beauty of the universe in a state of innocence, while in the fourth book, completed by William of Melitona after 1255, it is affirmed, at least in an appendix or scholion to the discussion of the *actual* function of the incarnation. Even if we bracket the fall, the author concludes, the incarnation would have been fitting, for then Christ would sanctify the whole of human nature and be encountered by man both within and outside himself. Albert the Great took the same position, on the grounds that the incarnation effects a *circulatio*, a return of the universe to its divine source.

Bonaventura, the chief representative of the Franciscan school after Alexander, produced his commentary on the *Sentences* in the early 1250s, before the fourth book of the *Summa* was written. He knew of all the arguments—the *circulatio* of God's works back to their origin, marriage as a sacrament of Christ and the Church, the accessibility of the Word both within and without. He acknowledged the supralapsarian view to be more in accord with the judgment of reason, but he thought the infralapsarian more in accord with the obedience of faith, since both the New Testament and the fathers mention only redemption as the motive of the incarnation. Taking Franciscan humility as his guide here as in other theological matters, he opted for faith rather than reason (*In IV Sent.*, d. 1, a. 2, q. 2). His view is that the incarnation is an overflowing (*excessus*) of divine mercy, in answer to an overflowing of rebellion against God. As for the argument that the incarnation brings the universe to its perfection, he answers that God ought not to be a factor *within* the perfection of the universe, for he is *above* all creaturely perfections. He is not like a king or leader who acts from within the host (*dux ex exercitu*), but more like one who

38. Victorin Doucet, "The History of the Problem of the Authenticity of the Summa," *Franciscan Studies*, VII (1947): 26–41, 274–312.

gives commands from above it (*dux supra exercitum* [*In III Sent.*, d. 1, a. 2, qq. 1–2]).

He also refers to a passage in which Bernard attacked Abelard, the *scrutator maiestatis*, for denying the redemptive purpose of the incarnation and asserting instead that it was simply "to illuminate the world with the light of his wisdom and kindle it to divine love" (*Tractatus de erroribus Abaelardi* [Ep. CXC], chaps. 5 and 9). The discussion in Bernard is not altogether convincing, for it seems to be an attempt to turn Abelard's theory of the influence exerted by Christ into a statement about the motive of the incarnation and then into an answer to the question what would have happened had Adam not sinned.[39] Still it is interesting to note that Bernard, and Bonaventura after him, saw a Pelagian tendency in this stress on the positive rather than the corrective function of the incarnation.

Thomas Aquinas, in his early commentary on the *Sentences* (*In III Sent.*, d. 1, q. 1, a. 3), viewed the motive of the incarnation as something that remains hidden in God's own will except insofar as it is revealed to men. He acknowledged both theories to be "probable," but then he went on to demolish the arguments put forward on both sides. Subsequently he turned decisively against the Christocentrist position. Once again he argued that the incarnation is a freely determined act of God, whose motive can be known only from revelation. When he consulted Scripture he found that the incarnation is always mentioned in connection with man's sin; therefore he had to conclude that it would not have taken place except for sin (*Summa Theologica*, III, q. 1, a. 3).

Despite this initial opposition, the Christocentrist doctrine that had been expressed in the fourth book of the *Summa fratris Alexandri* and in Albert's commentary on the *Sentences* became widespread in the last decades of the thirteenth century.[40] Its popularity doubtless helped to incline Scotus toward that opinion, but it should be noted that Scotus, far from passively accepting the doctrine in its received form, set it in an essentially new framework.

Scotus' views, which had such an influence on the subsequent discus-

---

39. A. Victor Murray, *Abelard and St. Bernard: A Study in Twelfth-Century "Modernism"* (Manchester: Manchester University Press, 1967), pp. 49–88, shows that Bernard based his indictment upon the *Capitula* drawn up by William of St. Thierry for the Council of Sens, and that neither of them had examined Abelard's own meaning very carefully.

40. Names are listed in North, *Teilhard*, pp. 143–44.

sion, are to be found in the two series of commentary on the *Sentences*, the earlier one called the *Opus Oxoniense* (which became in the sixteenth century the standard Scotist textbook) and the much shorter resumé and supplement called the *Reportata Parisiensia*. In both cases the manuscript does not come entirely from his own hand and may be overlaid with the attempts of his disciples to fill out the discussion. But it was of course the written works, not his oral instruction, that influenced later theologians.[41] The basic position is laid down in the Oxford lectures:

> it does not seem that God predestined [the soul of Christ] to so high a glory merely for the sake of [redemption], because redemption, the glorification of the soul that is to be redeemed, is not as great a good as the glory of the soul of Christ. It is not likely either that this highest good among created beings should be something that is merely "occasioned," that is, one that exists for the sake of a lesser good, or that God would predestine Adam before Christ, even though the predestining of Christ would then follow; indeed, there would be an even more absurd consequence, namely, that God, in predestining Adam to glory, would foresee Adam's fall into sin before he predestined Christ to glory if it were the case that the soul of Christ were predestined only for the sake of the redemption of others, for there would be no redemption unless a fall or trespass had preceded it. (*In III Sent.*, d. 7, q. 3, *dubia*)[42]

This passage indicates Scotus' basic concern, which is *not* to answer the purely speculative question what would have happened if Adam had not fallen, but to give a proper account of the structure of God's decrees in relation to the actual course of events. In the Paris lectures he sketches this in detail (*Reportata*, III, d. 7): God primarily loves himself; then this love is also extended beyond himself in the decision to create; third, he wills to be loved by another being which is outside himself; then, in order to achieve this, he wills the union of humanity with deity in the incarnation; and finally he foresees sin and decrees the redemptive death of Christ.[43] The point is therefore that God's

---

41. Some indication of the problems involved can be gained from North's discussion, pp. 144–46, and the literature cited there.

42. I am using the Lyons edition of 1639, recently reprinted (Hildesheim: Georg Olms Verlag, 1968).

43. P. Raymond, "Duns Scot," *Dictionnaire de théologie catholique*, IV. 2, cols. 1890–91.

overarching intention is to bring human nature to share in his own glory through its freely enacted love toward him, and the only appropriate way for this to occur, given the hierarchy of values with which Scotus is operating, is for God to will the incarnation prior to and apart from any consideration of sin.

In the heyday of scholasticism, by which I mean the seventeenth century, when the whole array of medieval theology and philosophy had been set down in print and the range of options was debated among theologians of many different persuasions, the Christocentrist position made steady advances, not only among Franciscans but among Jesuits and even among Dominicans.[44] It should be noted that there is an important difference in the *reasons* given by the Scotists and by the Thomists. The Scotists characteristically stressed God's subjective purposes and their formal sturcturing into a kind of realm of ideas, and they followed the dictum that what is last in the "order of execution" is the first and overarching aim in the "order of intention." The Thomists, even when they took up the Scotists' thesis, stated it in a different way. Their style of thought stressed the interconnected course of events in the one actual world-order, with God set above it, infallibly knowing and willing it as an organic whole, in one undivided act. Where the Scotists would tend to see the incarnation in terms of God's positive intentions for the completion of his purposes in creation (to which the redemptive function could then be added at a lower rank in the hierarchy of aims), the Thomists would tend to see God's will reflected directly in the actual texture of events, in which the work of redemption has an irreducible place. The difference comes out clearly in a number of recent Catholic theologians who have been writing on the motive for the incarnation.[45] Stressing as they do the redemptive aspects of the incarnation and refusing to speak of anything else than the definitive will of God, they remain Thomist rather than Scotist in their perspective, despite their concessions to Christocentrism.

---

44. Cf. Émile Mersch, *The Theology of the Mystical Body*, trans. Cyril Vollert (St. Louis: Herder, 1951), pp. 136–51; Hans Küng, *Justification: The Doctrine of Karl Barth and a Catholic Reflection* (London: Burn & Oates, 1964), pp. 129–40, 156–62, 272–88.

45. Cf. Mersch, *The Theology of the Mystical Body*, pp. 137–43; Hans Urs von Balthasar, *Karl Barth: Darstellung und Deutung seiner Theologie* (Olten: Hegner-Bücherei, 1951), pp. 335–37; Küng, *Justification*, pp. 123–70, 285–301; Felix Malmberg, *Über den Gottmenschen* (Quaestiones Disputatae, IX; Freiburg: Herder, 1960), pp. 11–13.

The Christocentrist theory was too speculative for the Reformers. Calvin attacked Osiander's view that Adam was created in the image of the incarnate Christ, and he painstakingly answered all the arguments that could be drawn from Scripture in defense of the view that the incarnation somehow has a place even apart from sin (*Institutes*, I, 15, 3; II, 12, 5–7). The same reserve was exhibited by the Lutheran and Reformed scholastics. The only analogue in the older Protestant theology to the Scotist position is supralapsarianism, the view held by a few of the Reformed theologians (Beza, Gomarus, and, in a mediating way, Maastricht), that God's most comprehensive decree is the manifestation of his mercy in the salvation of those elected in Christ and the manifestation of his justice in the damnation of those who are abandoned to their own sin. These theologians, with their interest in the hierarchical structure or "order of intention" in God's decrees, have obviously been influenced by the reading of Scotus. But the prevailing view, even among the Reformed, held to the sequence of events in the biblical narrative, and in its stress on the actual course of events it is akin to the thinking of Thomas—and of Calvin.[46]

The difference between the Scotist and the Thomist perspectives on God's willing helps us, I think, to point up the fundamental intentions on each side. It also exposes a dilemma that they faced together because they had to assume that the actual course of events, from creation to eschaton, is known and willed from eternity. The Scotists wished to emphasize God's purposiveness, transcending all that is actual or will ever be actual, and in the spirit of Anselm they also wished to show that this purposiveness is supremely coherent and wise; but in order to trace God's purposes they felt compelled to retroject the actual course of events into eternity, extrapolate from what faith says of the actual function and dignity of Christ to the contents of God's eternal decrees, and suppose that it was refined there down to the last detail. The Thomists wished to keep everything focused upon the texture of actual events; but in order to do this they had to conceive of God as, in effect, also narrowing his field of attention to that

---

46. For the debate among the Reformed theologians, see Heinrich Heppe, *Reformed Dogmatics Set Out and Illustrated from the Sources*, trans. G. T. Thomson (London: Allen & Unwin, 1950), pp. 146–49, 159–62, and also *CD*, II/2, 127–45, where Barth, with typical vigor, plays off the two positions against each other and ends by radicalizing the supralapsarian position in a Christocentrist direction.

same texture of events, eternally known and willed. Under the circumstances the most daring and courageous line of thought was not that of the speculative Christocentrists but that of the main body of theologians, for they were prepared to say that, even though Christ may now be the decisive turning point and the axis along which healing and renewal must take place, he was *not* that in God's antecedent intention. They were even willing to postulate a major readjustment in God's purposes following upon his foreknowledge of sin, so that the incarnation became a contingent measure, a means to the final attainment of God's antecedent aim.

The dilemma can be avoided if we abandon the conception of God's eternity as a simultaneous presence to all moments of time. Then we can have both the Thomists' healthy respect for the place of finite freedom, and secondary causes generally, in the course of events, and the Scotists' interest in the purposes of God—world-transcending, coherent, and now open and adaptable as well. In order to see how this can be done, it will be profitable to look at two important phases of modern theology, the first of them the "archetype Christology" of the classical period of German idealism, the other the attempt to find the place of Christ in an evolving world, both of which recognize the difficulty of making God's purposes the direct and specific cause of all the vicissitudes of history and the cosmos.

CHAPTER II

The Archetype Christology

We are all of us children of the nineteenth century in theology, even those who occasionally engage in parricide. It is always something of a surprise, after reading in the major twentieth-century theologians (especially the German ones), to discover how much they depend upon the thinkers of the classic period around 1800 and following—not so much in their particular assertions, for these can be quite variable, but in the language they speak, the problems they address, the range of possibilities they think of. Even a Barth, whose reputation is chiefly that of a fierce critic of the preceding era in theology, is dependent on it in many ways, finding in it not only a convenient target for his attacks but a standpoint from which to rebound to an opposing position, and even a source of insights which he gladly appropriates. The nineteenth century is still with us as part of our living past, then, and in understanding it we can understand ourselves better.

These comments apply especially to the question we are pursuing, the relation of Jesus to the human race or the relation of Christology to anthropology. That era is the source of many of the notions that are still bandied about, whether positively or negatively, in theological discussions of this question—and properly, for Christology was perhaps the central theme in the theology of that era: not Christology in its narrowly technical sense alone (although that was also involved), but Christology in its relationship with a more general understanding of human life; not anthropology pure and simple, however, but anthropology carried out in relation to an "archetypal ideal of humanity" which is made the basis of the link between Christ and others. In that era the fragmentary discussions and scattered insights that we have been examining were for the first time pulled together and discussed in a coherent way.

The occasion will come (in the fourth section of this chapter) for a glance at the full-scale debate that arose in the 1830s over the kinds of questions we have been tracing, namely, whether the incarnation is the preestablished goal and completion of human life before God or is rather the sequel to human failure, and, indeed, whether incarnation is possible at all. But the rules of that debate had already been set by the development of what I shall call the "archetype Christology," the view that Jesus is in some way the manifestation or actualization of the archetypal ideal for all humanity. Since that Christology was developed by the three giants who shaped the subsequent theology of the nineteenth and twentieth centuries, Kant, Schleiermacher, and Hegel, we must turn first to them, trying to bring out the chief insights of each into Christology and especially into the relationship of Jesus to others. Each made a major contribution, and it will be necessary for us to give sustained attention to the line of inquiry that was followed in each case.

To set them within a theological frame of reference we can perhaps classify them according to the articles of the Creed (understood as referring to the economy of salvation and the standpoint taken within it). In Kant we find a "Christology of the first article," in the sense that he was concerned with the general relationship of man to God and linked his Christology with an ideal to which all are called, juxtaposing this ideal, however, with their failure to come up to it, and stressing, as a consequence, their need for justification. In Schleiermacher we find a "Christology of the second article," in that he tried to give an account of the Christian consciousness as a specific feeling of dependence upon Jesus of Nazareth as the unique actualization of the ideal and denied the possibility of ever going beyond this direct dependence upon Jesus. In Hegel we find a "Christology of the third article," in that he emphasized, as against Kant, the transformation that can occur in human life, the real reconciliation with God and the real participation in the divine life that can come into being, and, as against Schleiermacher, the necessity of its occurring in each individual life and with a certain independence of the historical figure of Jesus. No judgment as to their relative merits is implied in this sequence; it is simply the order into which the materials fall. While each succeeding thinker will add some concerns which had been overlooked by the preceding ones, we shall not expect them to come to a grand synthesis in Hegel. They have probed three different dimensions of the Christian situation, and each has an indispensable contribution to make, a contribution that I shall try in each case to extract and preserve.

But perhaps we should first remind ourselves of the context in which they worked, immersing ourselves in the spirit of their times (just as we shall try once again to extricate ourselves from it in the fifth section of this chapter). From the start they were aware of a difficulty. Much of the biblical story was not only difficult to confirm from historical evidence; it was incredible as historical narrative to men who had a scientific knowledge of the way nature and human life go. One could not believe that the first human beings were named Adam and Eve and lived some four to five thousand years b.c. Many miracles and prophecies had to go by the board. Much that was believed about Jesus, and about the future course of cosmic history, and about many other things, became problematical. Indeed, the Bible itself, under careful scrutiny, turned out to speak with many different voices. These were not new problems. They had been aired by a few freethinkers during the seventeenth century, and they had come to be recognized more widely during the eighteenth century; but they remained a matter of esoteric knowledge among the literate classes, and there was no compulsion to deal with them as a serious problem. They gained notoriety and became unavoidable, it would seem, with the publication of the so-called "Wolfenbüttel Fragments" (actually seven lengthy extracts, of several hundred pages each, from a four-thousand-page manuscript left by Hermann Reimarus at his death), issued by Lessing between 1774 and 1778 under the fiction that he had come across them in the course of his work as librarian at Wolfenbüttel, the court of the Duke of Braunschweig. It was probably this more than anything that gave impetus to a new surge of interest in historical study of the Bible—and to a different line of attack upon the problem of understanding and justifying Christianity.

Since assertions about matters in the past are always open to doubt, or, if not that, at least to reinterpretation in a variety of ways, they cannot, by themselves, be an adequate basis of faith. In any event, to put the argument in a positive vein, true religion is something more than mere belief that certain things happened in the past. This was their point of departure. It is not that the historical process is unimportant—all these men, in their different ways, took it quite seriously. What they meant is that religious faith goes beyond mere knowledge or opinion about events in the past: whatever is said must have some pertinence to the believer in the present. They could quote Luther and many other writers to the same effect, that it is not enough to know *about* God or Christ but there must be some awareness of their importance "to me." Thus an aspect of subjectivity will quite naturally be central to their theological method, not as though they were ready to cut themselves loose from all controls and indulge their prejudices and impulses, but at least with the insistence that, *whatever* one is going to say, it must have some relationship to the subjectivity of the believer; and this is not a hard bargain. There is a wide selection of methods to follow, and in one way or another it is possible to take the point of view of the human subject and then move beyond mere subjectivity in a carefully controlled way.

Their perspective can be called, quite accurately, "rationalist" (it was so designated in their own age), and it is an outgrowth of the rationalism of the earlier eighteenth century. It is characteristically embarrassed about the "positive," the merely factual and thus seemingly arbitrary features of the biblical tradition, and therefore it attempts to exhibit Christianity as the one purely rational and universally valid religion. In the process it is willing to abandon, if necessary, the whole of the Old Testament as a mere preparatory stage and to reformulate potentially every part of the Christian message in order to bring out its reasonableness the more effectively. The shortcomings of such an approach will be obvious—an excessive eagerness to show that Christianity is equivalent with the latest fashions in the intellectual world, a cavalier attitude toward the importance of historical events, a condescending judgment upon the Jews as adherents of a primitive and hopelessly obsolescent faith. We shall have occasion to chastise them as we go along and to offer a corrected formulation of their insights. But these mistakes and abuses may still be only incidental to their "rationalist" approach; at least we should give them the benefit of the doubt. What is more worth noting is that the impulse is not an unusual one in Christian thought, and its most evident parallel is to be found in the Church fathers (or at least many among them, and the most influential), who were also concerned to show that the biblical message converged with the best philosophy of the age, sometimes correcting it, to be sure, but also finding in it many appropriate forms of expression and ways of relating faith to general human experience. I hope that it will become clear as I go along how similar the assumptions and patterns of thinking are.

The chief difficulty for most eighteenth-century German thinkers was to account for the concrete particularity of Jesus; but this was the result not of the drive toward rationality and general validity but of a difficulty in relating the rational to the historical. It must be noted from the start that what they were doing was never a confident attempt to characterize the "real" Jesus as he was in himself; they were too well apprised of the difficulties of both the historical and the dogmatic methods to attempt that. Instead they were looking at the meaning of Jesus for other persons, or for the believing community, or for humanity in general, and they knew that their point of departure in doing this must be the human consciousness, not Jesus in himself, who remained problematical. They were not necessarily skeptical about the possibility of knowing the real Jesus (although a few of them were). But they recognized that the Christian Church had always stressed the significance of Jesus for others, and the rise of historical and dogmatic problems, far from making that emphasis obsolete, had given the occasion for a more careful inquiry into what that significance actually is. Some of them, it is true, concluded that Jesus' significance lay chiefly in what was mistakenly attributed to him by others. But some would hear of no other theory than that the belief arose because of what Jesus really was. Still others thought that they could make reliable statements about Jesus himself on the basis of the way others were related to him. What joins all of them together and makes modern German theology, despite its family quarrels, a single movement is that they operate in terms of a correlation between the meaning of Christ and the human consciousness, stressing sometimes one pole and sometimes the other, but never separating them. Their statements float in this atmosphere of mutual relationship, neither being reduced to a pure subjectivity devoid of broader reference nor becoming anchored firmly in undisputed reality. This limitation justifies, in a sense, the rival attempt to get beyond their methods and reach some firm convictions about the real state of affairs, whether through dogmatics or metaphysics or historical study or some combination of them. But we also know that their critique of previous attempts to gain "objective truth" or "knowledge of reality" in Christology was justified. It is safe to say that whatever theological convictions about the "real Jesus" we may arrive at will be the outcome of a long process of testing our hypotheses against theirs to see which combination makes the best fit with the historical data, the testimonies of faith and dogma, and the rational structures of metaphysics.

Therefore when we approach the epoch-making German thinkers we must take their thought for what it is, a cautious investigation of the language of Christology, executed chiefly by looking backward at the inherited beliefs of the Christian community and cautioning anyone who looked ahead toward new assertions that the conditions of knowledge are under severe constraints. What we must expect of them, then, is a phenomenological account of the meaning of Christ in traditional Christianity, an attempt to salvage this meaning, in the face of all the difficulties, by relating it explicitly and completely to current experience, and a preliminary exploration of the language with which christological assertions about the "real Jesus" might be made.

I. Kant and the "Ideal of Humanity"

The Kant with whom we have to deal is not the one made familiar to us by the conventional lectures and writings in the history of philosophy, based on the three *Critiques*, but the Kant of *Religion within the Limits of Reason Alone*, generally overlooked or insufficiently plumbed in most treatments.[1] Religion was a problem which had exercised him for a long time, and he explored it thoroughly and with a characteristic rejection of humbug and mere "edification."

It was a long pilgrimage.[2] Kant had been born and brought up in

---

1. The first of the four "books" was published in the *Berlinische Monatsschrift* in 1792; subsequent parts were refused permission by the censor, and Kant published the whole work separately, with an imprimatur from the philosophical faculty at Jena, in 1793. He added a number of footnotes and another preface for the second edition of 1794.

2. For the religious milieu of Königsberg and the influences on Kant, see Benno Erdmann, *Martin Knutzen und seine Zeit. Ein Beitrag zur Geschichte der wolfischen Schule und insbesondere zur Entwicklungsgeschichte Kants* (Leipzig: Voss, 1876) and Georg Hollmann, "Prolegomena zur Genesis der Religionsphilosophie Kants," *Altpreussische Monatsschrift*, XXXI (1899):1–73. The definitive study of the influences reflected in the *Religion*, traced in minute detail, is Josef Bohatec, *Die Religionsphilosophie Kants in der "Religion innerhalb der Grenzen der*

Königsberg, and he enrolled in the faculty of theology at the university there. He soon turned away from the prospect of a career in the clergy, being dismayed at the "hypocrisy" of the pietists; but he seems to have retained a spontaneous interest in theology. One of his biographers, Borowski, says that in a bookstore Kant once encountered a student of his buying a book on religion and mentioned that years before he had read thoroughly Stapfer's *Grundlegung zur wahren Religion*.[3] Since the work in question was published 1746–1753, Kant's interest manifestly continued beyond his years as a student in the faculty of theology. Although he forswore all external practice of religion, even prayer, as his associates knew well, he was not a scoffer of the sort familiar in the French Enlightenment; he thought such people frivolous. He had his own intensely demanding moral code, and, beyond that, a religion of moral responsibility which he viewed as a properly reformed version of Christianity, far superior to the nearest philosophical rival, Stoicism. He offered a course of lectures on "philosophical theology" in the early 1780s (following the publication of the *Critique of Pure Reason* in 1781, it will be noted). In these lectures, later published from student notes,[4] and in his extensive comments in a handwritten copy of lectures on natural theology by Eberhard of Halle in 1781[5] we can trace the beginning of a new surge of interest in religious questions, now thoroughly within the framework of the critical philosophy. Bohatec has shown in his massive study that Kant kept up with the writings of at least some of his more important contemporaries.[6]

---

blossen Vernunft." Mit besonderer Berücksichtigung ihrer theologisch-dogmatischen Quellen (Hamburg: Hoffman und Campe, 1938). The background of scholastic philosophy is traced in Lewis White Beck, *Early German Philosophy: Kant and His Predecessors* (Cambridge, Mass.: Harvard University Press, 1969). For Kant's subsequent controversies during the 1790s in their eighteenth-century context, see Wilhelm Dilthey, "Der Streit Kants mit der Zensur über das Recht freier Religionsforschung," *Gesammelte Schriften*, IV (Leipzig and Berlin: Teubner, 1921), 285–309.

3. *Immanuel Kant. Ein Lebensbild nach Darstellung der Zeitgenossen Jachmann, Borowski, Wasianski*, ed. Alfons Hoffmann (Halle: Hugo Peter, 1902), p. 253 (in the original, printed in Königsberg in 1804, pp. 171–72).

4. *Vorlesungen über die philosophische Religionslehre*, hrsg. Karl Heinrich Ludwig Pölitz (Leipzig, 1817 and 1830).

5. Reprinted in *Kant's Gesammelte Schriften*, hrsg. von der Preussischen Akademie der Wissenschaften ("Akademie-Ausgabe"), XVIII, 489–606.

6. Bohatec, *Die Religionsphilosophie Kants*, pp. 19–32 and 41–60, lists Reimarus, Lessing, Semler, Michaelis, and Staüdlin, along with a few older and more traditional writers.

In the *Religion* we can expect to find Kant, therefore, in his function as a theologian, left-handed though it may be, for he will manifest the influence of his Christian milieu and he will be attempting, as he himself hints toward the end of the second preface, to present a kind of catechism for the more reasonable form of religion that he hoped would eventually supplant the clericalism he saw too often around him. The method of the work, as the preface to the second edition states explicitly (the drafts for it are even clearer), is to seek out the purely rational elements in Christianity. This does not mean that he was attempting to construct a religion "out of" (*aus*) pure reason, in a synthetic or deductive fashion (he had already made some attempts in this direction in the *Critique of Practical Reason* and knew that they did not get very far); rather, accepting "revealed religion" as it stands, he decided to proceed analytically and inquire about those elements of it which are "within" (*innerhalb*) the limits of pure reason.[7] He uses the illustration of two concentric circles. Because the outer one (revealed religion) encloses the inner one (rational religion) it is possible to approach much of the former from the standpoint of the latter.

We should not be surprised, then, when Kant makes use of Christian doctrines and vocabulary throughout the work, but either rephrases them according to the requirements of pure reason or identifies articles of faith which, even though they are outside the range of moral reason, are in accord with it. We must be patient enough to follow him through a long course of reasoning and not come immediately to tag-phrases like "moral ideal" or "kingdom of God" which too often are all that the textbooks on theology convey of Kant's thought. His position is complex, and the "archetype Christology" which he developed rests on other assertions that must be traced first. Kant's importance to theology is precisely in his developing a "Christology" that claims to be able to dispense with the person of Jesus altogether; it is a radically "anthropological" approach to theology, and we must let him build his case.

Calling forth Goethe's remark that Kant had soiled his philosopher's robe, the first book announced a theme that astonished his contemporaries, for they had not seen the anticipations of it in his previous writings: "Concerning the Indwelling of the Evil Principle with the Good, or, On the Radical Evil in Human Nature." It is not only an impressive,

7. See the drafts for the second preface in *Lose Blätter*, III, 59 and 90–92.

and subsequently influential, attempt to rethink the doctrine of bondage to sin, a bondage whose origins are out of sight in the dim beginnings of his activity of willing; it is important to Kant philosophically, as the outcome of a lengthy inquiry into the nature and the incentives of willing.[8]

In speaking of "radical evil," Kant does not want to suggest that everything we will or do is unambiguously evil. In fact, one of his achievements was to think through the problem very carefully and get away from any simplistic notion of total depravity, for it is obvious that we are aware of what is good and often do it, at least to all external appearances. His point is that in the struggle between their discernment of the good and their anxieties or desires, the latter turn out to be the controlling "incentives" of the will, even when good deeds are done. For good deeds may be done from unworthy motives, and this, while it indicates the presence of both good and evil tendencies within man, confirms the doctrine of "radical evil." Let us see, then, what explanation he can offer.

Kant thinks that man has and retains a natural "predisposition" (*Anlage*) toward the good—toward good character, personhood in its proper sense—in his capacity to make decisions solely out of respect for the dictates of practical reason (*Rel*, pp. 22–23; *AA*, VI, 27–28). But there is a difference between *Willkür* (*arbitrium*, choice), the ability to make decisions with respect to concrete actions, choosing between the possible alternatives, and *Wille* (*voluntas*, will), the ability to determine, on the basis of the law of reason alone, the fundamental stance that will be adopted, the maxims or basic principles that will be followed, in making those concrete decisions. "Choice" is freedom in the ordinary sense, and because it is in contact with all the data that are pertinent to action, it is easily affected by passion and impulse. True freedom, however, can come only from the capacity of "will" to respond to moral reason, with its demand for total consistency in all actions (*Metaphysic of Morals*, *AA*, VI, 213–14). It consists, negatively, in freedom from the constraints of impulse and passion, and, positively, in making practical reason the sole foundation of action in such a way

8. See especially the excellent introductory essay by John R. Silber in the Torchbook edition of the *Religion*, which analyzes the crucial notions of *Wille*, *Willkür*, and *Gesinnung*. On p. cx he indicates the importance of Book I in Kant's own philosophical development.

that "will" perfectly determines, and reflects itself in, the specific acts of "choice." All of this is obviously in continuity with the Stoic and especially the Augustinian conception of freedom, probably as handed on to Kant through the textbooks used in instruction.

In the crucial position between the capabilities of "will" and the everyday exercise of "choice" Kant introduces the important notion of "disposition" (*Gesinnung*). It is what is meant by more ordinary terms (also used by Kant) such as "character" or "the heart." The proof of the role of disposition is the fact that people do not respond to *every* value, *every* object that accosts them, but they are selective; indeed, they may be entirely unresponsive to some objects or some aspects of them. They act "true to character," as we say, in the exercise of their free choice, according to some fundamental orientation, and even when there is a variety of motives or dispositions one of them will be dominant. A disposition is determinative of all that one will value and pursue, and it is so resistant to change that it is in effect ineradicable. Yet man himself is no less responsible for it. Kant must conclude that the taking up of a disposition is an act of "choice" itself, though of a privileged kind, preceding and determining all subsequent acts of choosing. Since it is not a concrete act in man's commerce with the spatio-temporal world, its locus must be the transcendental freedom in which decisions are made solely in relation to the law of reason (*Rel*, pp. 20–21, 26; *AA*, VI, 25–26, 31).

But how is it that man, who has a natural predisposition toward good character and is capable of bringing all his animal desires and his self-centered anxieties under the control of moral reason, succumbs to temptation? Kant, using at least in a figurative way the language of Platonism, likes to describe man as standing between two "worlds," two spheres or dimensions of life, the intelligible world in which moral reason ought to shape his self-commitments as a person, and the natural world, operating according to its iron laws of physical necessity, to which man is bound by the many ties of need and anxiety, impulse and affection. Kant assumes that in the earliest stages of human history, when people were not merely untrained in the use of reason but totally unaware of it, they would inevitably give in to impulse and self-seeking; reason and will would not assert themselves independently but would develop first as the servants of the passions and only gradually arrive at a sense of moral obligation and acquire the incentive to improve (for this, see especially the *Vorlesungen*, pp. 150–52, and the whole section, pp. 149–57). Thus Kant reopens the question about man's primitive state and the sources of original sin, a question that had been closed in late antiquity after the Origenist and Pelagian controversies, and he answers it in a new way that will influence all subsequent theologians.

When Kant sets about giving a psychological account of the process, applicable to each individual, he suggests that a "propensity toward evil" grows by subtle stages—first as mere frailty, giving in to the incentives of animality or egoism despite the intention to follow a better policy; then as improbity, a failure of integrity, a kind of ambiguous thinking and ambivalent willing that harbors the illusion of virtue but acts from other motives; and finally as depravity, a propensity to adopt policies which simply ignore the moral law (*Rel*, pp. 21–27, 31–34; *AA*, VI, 26–32, 36–39; cf. Silber, pp. cxxi–cxxvii). The moral law still stands, and the natural capacity of the will to respond to it remains; but the gap between expectation and achievement serves only to demonstrate man's guilt and his inability to reverse the propensity toward evil. In order to reverse that tendency man would have to adopt wholeheartedly a policy of doing good; but his fundamental orientation is already opposed to this, and consequently he cannot make such a decision. The question of redemption therefore arises from within the life of sinful man. Somehow there must be a change in the fundamental disposition of the will, a "revolution" in the heart, a reversal of commitments.

But how is this flip-over to be accomplished? Kant rejects any attempt to introduce the notion of prevenient grace (understood as a special divine impulse) at this point (*Rel*, pp. 47–49; *AA*, VI, 52–53). Instead, he simply sets before men their own high destiny as moral beings and the numinous quality of the moral task—what he himself will term the call of the holy Lawgiver. The classic passage, of course, is the apostrophe in the *Critique of Practical Reason*—"Duty! Thou sublime and mighty name!"—whose point is that the moral law brings before man the sublimity of his own vocation to moral integrity and, by calling to his attention the unworthiness of his conduct, arouses a deeper respect for this high calling (*PR*; *AA*, V, 86–89). In the *Religion within the Limits of Reason Alone* there are two similar passages which illuminate Kant's thinking:

> There is one thing in our soul which we cannot cease regarding with
> the highest wonder, when we view it properly, and for which admira-
> tion is not only legitimate but even exalting, and that is the original
> moral predisposition itself in us. . . . the very incomprehensibility of this
> predisposition, which announces a divine origin, acts perforce upon the
> spirit even to the point of exaltation, and strengthens it for whatever
> sacrifice a man's respect for his duty [his sublime moral destiny] may
> demand of him. (*Rel*, pp. 44–45; *AA*, VI, 49–50)

> This is the key to the overcoming of radical evil. The corruption
> can be overcome only through the idea of moral goodness in its entire
> purity, together with the consciousness that this idea really belongs to
> our original predisposition and that we need but be assiduous in pre-
> serving it free from all impure admixture and in registering it deeply in
> our dispositions to be convinced, by its gradual effect upon the spiritual
> nature, that the dreaded powers of evil can in no wise make headway
> against it . . . . (*Rel*, p. 78; *AA*, VI, 83)

It is worth reflecting theologically on this for a moment. Kant seems
at first glance (and probably seemed to himself) defiantly semi-Pe-
lagian, attributing the beginning of conversion to man himself and
giving to divine assistance a role (if it has any role at all) only subsequently, as cooperating with and strengthening man's will. But he is
not so far from a major tradition of Christian theology as he supposed.
Augustine and many of those who have followed him would agree that
"divine assistance" (the grace of the Holy Spirit) is given after conversion to strengthen man's good will and good purposes, and they would
say that the factor which precedes conversion is an influence that
comes to the will not directly but indirectly, by presenting inducements through the intellect.[9] In Kant this converting power is the quality of holiness or unconditionedness in the moral law, testifying to its
divine origin. It is not a casual matter, for here we are at the focal
point of his entire theology and Christology, such as it is. He often
speaks, even in earlier writings (cf. *PR*; *AA*, V, 83–84) of the "ideal of
holiness" to which men are called, the "archetype" or pattern which is
held before them and to which their moral disposition ought to conform. In the *Religion* he says that "the idea itself, which reason presents to us for our zealous emulation, can give us power" for its own
fulfillment. This it can do because of its divine origin, signaled by its

---

9. This assertion is substantiated, I trust, in my study *Augustine the Theologian*
(New York: Herder & Herder, 1970), pp. 161–65, 201–4, 332–34.

perfection, so different from the finitude and unworthiness of man. Kant even equates it with the Word or Son of God, in a more or less plausible modification of the Trinitarian doctrine (although perhaps it would be better to forget it and simply speak of the "archetypal ideal of humanity"), since he thinks that the idea of "a humanity well-pleasing to God," corresponding to his own holiness, is the content of God's eternal decree—that is, the goal of all his purposes, and even his reason for creating a world at all (*Rel*, p. 54; *AA*, VI, 60)—and thus can be called "God's all-sustaining Idea, the archetype of humanity, begotten by himself" (*Rel*, p. 136; *AA*, VI, 145 [translation mine]).

What Kant means by an "ideal" is spelled out in the *Critique of Pure Reason* (A 312–20, A 567–83). He wants to retain the traditional term *idea*, and even to use it as Plato used it, though with the hope of understanding him better than he understood himself. An idea is a "concept of reason" which transcends all experience. An *ideal*, beyond this, is a *fully individuated* concept, determined in every detail by ideas alone (A 567–68). It is well known that Kant found difficulty with the *theoretical* employment of ideas. One can, for example, form a conception of God as the supreme "ideal of pure reason," and this ideal can have important functions in our thinking about metaphysical problems, but it remains only an ideal and there is no guarantee that it has reference to a real being. But Kant, taking his clue from one aspect of the Platonist tradition, thinks that ideas, and fully individuated "ideals," can have a *practical* use as "regulative principles," as points of reference by which to judge those things that are experienced. He is unwilling to go so far as Plato in spinning out a theory of ideas in the divine understanding which are the archetypes producing things within the field of experience, for this would involve a speculative theory which cannot be tested (A 568–69). But there is one exception. An ideal produced by pure reason *can* be used in the *moral* life, and the ideal of humanity in its total perfection can even be affirmed (though only by practical reason) to be an idea in God's mind, indeed, the idea in accordance with which he himself creates and rules the world. This ideal presides over human life from the beginning, first only as a demand that projects a possibility for human life, then perhaps as an efficacious power steadily making good its claims. But there is no guarantee that it will be actualized, although of course it *ought* to be actualized. As Kant puts it in one place, the final goal of all things is a humanity *subject to* moral laws, but to say that they will assuredly live *in accordance* with moral laws is to go beyond anything we can know of the power of the Creator and, in addition, to contravene human freedom (*Critique of Judgment; AA*, V, 448–49 and n.). Its actualization must come, then, not by divine interference but through free human enactment. But Kant thinks he can show how the ideal can arouse, and sustain, and even validate, the requisite human enactment. It goes in three stages.

The ideal of a humanity well-pleasing to God demands of the individual a holiness that corresponds to God's own holiness. God is holy, his will is morally perfect, and it is impossible for him to will what is not in accordance with moral reason, since the willing of the good is natural to him. But when it comes to man, holiness, the doing of the good gladly, is only an "ideal" to be striven for, since man's will remains finite, distinct from goodness itself. Yet God as holy Lawgiver makes his unconditional demands in spite of the finitude and frailty, even the total failure, of man. This will be the first of those "mysteries" concerning God's action which Kant finds suggested by the Christian religion, that man is not merely created but is also *called*, as a free and rational being, to citizenship in God's kingdom (*Lose Blätter*, II, 184–87; *Rel*, pp. 129–38; *AA*, VI, 137–47).

But this calling, this unconditional demand, can only intensify the problem. The best that can be expected of man is not holiness but "virtue," by which Kant means a constant struggle and self-conquest, at best an unending progress toward holiness (*Vorlesungen*, p. 146; *PR; AA*, V, 31–33, 81–84). Yet that very drama is what makes human life interesting, and Kant likes to quote from a poem of Albrecht von Haller,

> . . . the world with all its failings still
> Is better than a host of angels void of will.
>   (*Metaphysic of Morals, AA*, VI, 397, n.;
>   *Rel.*, 58 n.; *AA*, VI, 65 n.)

The theme is examined in a magnificent section of the *Critique of Practical Reason* on the "incentives" of the moral life. Because we are embodied, sensory beings, our first experience, he suggests there, is always a desire or fear directed toward particular things and situations, and thus there is a propensity toward selfishness (the satisfaction of these impulses) and even toward arrogance and willfulness (a total dominance over one's surroundings). The moral reason, or its embodiment in righteous persons whom we know, stands in judgment over this propensity to selfishness and willfulness, frustrates it, causes pain, humiliates us when we compare ourselves with what is demanded of us. This is what gives rise to the feeling that Kant calls "respect" (*Achtung*) or "reverence" (*Verehrung*) for the moral demand or toward the righteous ones who exemplify it. As a feeling it belongs to our affective life, and it is a negative feeling of frustration, pain, humiliation. But since the whole character of this feeling has been shaped by the moral law conveyed through practical reason it is an incentive to the life of moral integrity (*PR; AA*, V, 72–76). The distinctive feature of this feeling is that the authority of the moral law is acknowledged even when it stands over against oneself in the mode of command, obligation, constraint, condemnation. It is not that the moral law is alien to man himself, for it is given to the will through man's own reason; only that there is a tension, built into the human condition, between the requirement of reason and the response of the will. Man does *not* follow the moral law spontaneously and gladly; he must do it out of humility and respect for the law, and *this* is what animates virtue.

Kant accuses Stoicism—even though it is in his estimate the highest achievement of moral philosophy in any age—of a premature resolution of the problem of the moral life, for it supposes that man can achieve complete rectitude of will and that he can find perfect happiness in it. The Stoics did not recognize the extent of the problem, he says, perhaps because they did not have the courage to acknowledge it. But the Christian commandment of love—something which, paradoxically, cannot be commanded in the strict sense, since it is a disposition to do the good spontaneously and gladly—this commandment, by its very difficulty, will not allow such "fantasies" of moral perfection: the demand is so exalted and uncompromising that man's self-confidence is destroyed, and hope of gaining true holiness of will is restored only in the promise of divine assistance (*PR; AA*, V, 86, 126–27, 127 n.). Furthermore, since men come to awareness of their proper destiny only after first succumbing to the temptations of embodied life, it is not easy to reestablish the proper hierarchy of incentives in the will. Kant therefore stresses the arduousness of human life, the continuing actuality of moral struggle, and heaps scorn upon the fanaticism or sentimentality of those who think they have achieved, or are capable of achieving, such steadfastness of heart that they will be spontaneously inclined to act with integrity, and also upon those who expect, through "edifying" exhortations or example, to induce men to lead a life of integrity, perhaps even to condition them to it or dupe them into it without their awareness (*PR*; *AA*, V, 81–86).

It is evident that Kant has been so struck by the Christian demand of holiness and promise of beatitude that he remains dissatisfied with all the conventional notions of the moral life. The moral law makes infinite demands that cannot be met by man himself. Although it is conceivable that man could always act *virtuously* in the midst of constant struggle, it is *not* conceivable that he could achieve, by himself, either *holiness* or the spiritual *happiness* that follows from it (*PR*; *AA*, V, 117–18), for even when there has been a "revolution" or "conversion" in the fundamental orientation of the will, so that virtue, with its progress toward holiness, replaces radical evil, the conflict between good and evil dispositions in man continues. What Kant is working with here is the Pauline-Augustinian-Lutheran acknowledgment of a tension, not only within the man who is striving to obey the law as mere external command (Romans 7), but even within the Christian, who has the "first fruits of the Spirit" but must still hope and strive for a complete victory over the power of sin (Romans 8). The difference between the enslaved and the liberated man is not that between total depravity and total righteousness, but that between being dominated by the evil "principle" or "disposition" in one's preferences and decisions, and being dominated by the good principle. All of this, worked out by Kant in dependence upon the writings of recent theologians,[10] is in keeping with the classic Christian understanding of man; indeed, it makes an important contribution to its more accurate formulation.

As we have seen, what is religiously important to Kant is the archetypal ideal of a humanity pleasing to God, a humanity having the disposition of perfect holiness. But when man first becomes aware of it, it is juxtaposed with his own imperfections. Therefore he cannot suppose that he himself is the ultimate source of this ideal, and he knows that it is set before him despite his own unworthiness and stands in judgment

---

10. Bohatec, *Die Religionsphilosophie Kants*, pp. 241–65, 327–39, traces the influence of Stapfer, Heilmann, and Michaelis, three academic theologians of the eighteenth century.

over him. Even when his basic disposition changes, so that he is dominated not by the evil principle but by the good, still he cannot suppose that it was he himself who set evil aside, that he raised himself toward the ideal of holiness. He will say rather that this archetype has "come down" to be united with sinful humanity (*Rel*, pp. 54–55; *AA*, VI, 60–61). Kant is using the theme of the incarnation of the Word as a parable for the internal struggle between an old humanity and a new, between the good disposition, already made dominant by the authority of the ideal, and the evil disposition, whose effects are still powerful. But the fact that it is made into a parable does not destroy its importance. The archetypal ideal has *not* been reduced to the status of a product of man himself, for it stands beyond all that he is or can become.

In view of human failure and its continuing effects even when men have made a basic reorientation, it is necessary, therefore, to postulate "satisfaction" (*Genugtuung*), that the shortcomings in their obedience be compensated by the perfection of the archetypal ideal (the "Son of God") toward which they are striving. The problem is this: God's favor or beneficence is not unconditioned but is rather conditioned upon their fulfillment of the task imposed upon them by the holiness of God, and they are unable to come up to that standard. It is obvious that something akin to justification by faith is needed, and it is a suitable accompaniment to God's holiness, as the necessary precondition of the completion of his own purposes. Kant does not want to base this justification or satisfaction in an atonement made by Christ, for he is not convinced that it could be applied to other individuals, and in any case human effort must also play a role. His solution is that there can be satisfaction, but that it comes about only *after* God has seen that the moral character of persons is fundamentally right. Then he counts them righteous despite their imperfect righteousness, for God not only knows the heart as man never can but also knows each life timelessly, in its total expanse, so that he can reckon it as righteous if there is progress in the struggle against sin. This, he says, is the second "mystery" suggested by Christianity (*Lose Blätter*, II, 184–87; *Rel*, pp. 129–38; *AA*, VI, 137–47).[11]

11. See especially Emanuel Hirsch, "Luthers Rechtfertigungslehre bei Kant," *Luther-Jahrbuch*, IV (1922): 47–65, and his later discussion in *Geschichte der neuern evangelischer Theologie im Zusammenhang mit der allgemeinen Bewegungen des europäischen Denkens*, IV (Gütersloh: C. Bertelsmann, 1952), 325–29.

Kant has not excluded all meaningful faith in Jesus. Atonement by another, he concedes, can be introduced as a "grace" that makes up what is lacking in man's own obedience; the only reservation he insists upon is that the bestowal of this grace must be conditioned upon a genuine obedience already within man (*Rel*, pp. 106–10; *AA*, VI, 116–20). This is in keeping with his principle that the point of departure must always be rational religion (the inner circle, that which is "within the limits of reason"). Then it is permissible to be open to revealed or positive or historical elements insofar as they *reinforce* or *supplement* the disposition toward good (*Rel*, p. 166; *AA*, VI, 178). Kant does not dispute the belief, furthermore, that Jesus is the one actual exemplification of the ideal in all its purity; indeed, he seems to affirm it, even as a part of his rational inquiry into religion, though with the caution that we cannot be entirely certain about centuries-old testimony, and that even Jesus' contemporaries could have gained only indirect knowledge of his inward disposition which is alleged to conform to the ideal (*Rel*, pp. 56–59; *AA*, VI, 63–65).

But what is it that we are to look for from Jesus? Not any new knowledge of the ideal of holiness, for it is always present to moral reason. Even when one believes that the ideal has been actualized in Jesus, it is the ideal *as apprehended by reason* that predominates and supplies the criterion for judgment. Its manifestation in history is secondary and is evaluated from the ideal.

> In the appearance of the God-man, it is not that in him which strikes the senses and can be known through experience, but rather the archetype lying in our reason and attributed to him (since, so far as his example can be known, he is found to conform thereto), which is really the object of saving faith . . . . (*Rel*, p. 110; *AA*, VI, 119)

The historical does not come into tension with the ideal in man's religious life, nor does it add anything to his moral awareness. There is simply the "one and the same practical idea," seen from two points of view, "now as found in God and proceeding from him, now as found in us" (ibid.).

The importance of Jesus must lie, therefore, in the realm not of knowledge but of practice. It is his unique honor to have achieved the decisive "revolution" in the history of the human race, for he breaks the hold of evil over the collective life of humanity and inaugurates a new collective life under a new ruling principle (*Rel*, pp. 74–77, 146–47; *AA*, VI, 79–82, 158–59). Even before Jesus the influence of the ideal could effect conversion in the hearts of men. But it is not enough to have an individual and merely private relationship with God, for the moral man will still find himself within an immoral society. It is at this point, then, that Kant introduces the idea of the kingdom of God, acknowledging its importance in the teachings of Jesus and linking it to the unique role of Jesus in human history—yet describing it in a way that once again, just as in the case of the archetypal ideal, robs Jesus of any indispensable or irreversible relationship to the ideal.

The kingdom of God is connected with the postulate of God as World Ruler, and this postulate completes the search for a "highest good," an actual state of affairs that can be sought as an end, for it guarantees the eventual convergence of virtue and happiness, morality and nature, individual and society (*PR*; *AA*, V, 129). The kingdom of God, and its anticipatory stage in a "people of God," is described as a commonwealth (as opposed to a state of nature), and as an ethical commonwealth (as opposed to political). It is a union of rational beings under laws of virtue, establishing conditions under which the good will of individuals will be encouraged rather than undermined, as it is in the common life generally. It is to be noted that the kingdom of God cannot, in Kant's thinking, be "merely" ethical. Whereas morality concerns what lies within the individual's power, the idea of an ethical commonwealth presupposes the idea of a moral deity through whose rule all are united into a whole (*Rel*, pp. 88–89; *AA*, VI, 96–98). So the kingdom of God is a *religious* idea, a hope which the morally committed person has the right to postulate beyond the bare demands of the moral law, and it must remain a kingdom *of God*, for it depends upon him as the only sufficient source of order and guarantee of achievement (*Rel*, pp. 90–91, 139; *AA*, VI, 98–99, 151). Since we cannot know how God will actualize it, the kingdom must remain, for us, a "Church invisible," a Platonic idea of all righteous persons united under a divine moral government, which can only be approximated in the life of a "people of God," although some such earthly "people," with its organized life, is indispensable as the representation and vehicle of the true ethical commonwealth (*Rel*, pp. 92–93; *AA*, VI, 101–2).

The importance of Jesus is that such a commonwealth—already conceived by practical reason—was for the first time put into effect in the

new people of God founded on Jesus' teachings and strengthened by
the moral victory of his obedience unto death. Consequently

> the dominion of the good principle begins, and a sign that "the king-
> dom of God is at hand" appears, as soon as the basic principles of its
> constitution first become *public*; for (in the realm of the understand-
> ing) that is already here whose causes, which alone can bring it to pass,
> have generally taken root, even though the complete development of its
> appearance in the sensuous world is still immeasurably distant. (*Rel*, p.
> 139; *AA*, VI, 151)

And yet the success of even this community is to be gauged by the
degree to which it directs people toward the pure and inward religion
of reason and progressively diminishes the element of external authority. The progress of the kingdom of God is in the last analysis parallel
with the progress of enlightenment, and it will reach its fruition with
the general recognition that divine revelation occurs in the medium of
moral reason, not in the world of sensory experience (*Rel*, pp. 112–13;
AA, VI, 121–22).

> "When, therefore, cometh the kingdom of God?" "The kingdom of God
> cometh not in visible form. Neither shall they say, Lo here, or lo there!
> *For behold, the kingdom of God is within you.*" (Luke 17:21–22).
> (*Rel*, p. 126; *AA*, VI, 136)

Thus everything ultimately returns to the structure of moral experience, and all the beneficent influences of God are to be found there.
Kant is quite serious about interpreting moral experience (or at least
its ultimate implications and the questions it raises) in a theistic way,
and it is here that he thinks he can discern the only sure meaning of
the "revealed mysteries" of Christianity—revealed because they are an
indisputable part of practical life, but still mysteries because their
application to God remains problematical from the standpoint of theoretical reason (*Rel*, p. 133; *AA*, VI, 141). The first of those "mysteries,"
as we have seen, is *calling*—God as holy Lawgiver continues to invite
persons, despite their failures, to citizenship in a moral kingdom. The
second is *satisfaction*—God as wise Ruler supplements their shortcomings out of the fullness of his own holiness, on the basis of their fundamental commitment to the ideal and their struggle with sin. The third
mystery closes the circle. It is *election*—God as righteous Judge makes

a definitive judgment upon all individuals. They are judged according to God's love if, out of respect for the Lawgiver, they have set themselves under the ideal and the good disposition predominates over the evil; then they can be considered God's own. Otherwise they fall into the hands of strict justice before an accusing conscience (*Rel*, pp. 136–37 n.; *AA*, VI, 145–46 n.).

Ultimately the three mysteries become one great mystery, arising out of the moral life with its numinous overtones. If the goal of human life consists of holiness, "love of the [eternal] law," then, Kant says,

> the equivalent of this idea in religion would be an article of faith: "God is love." In him we can revere the one who loves (with the love of moral approbation toward men insofar as they measure up to his holy law), the *Father*; further, insofar as he expresses himself in his all-sustaining Idea, the archetype of humanity begotten and beloved by him, his *Son*; and finally, insofar as he restricts this approbation according to man's correspondence with the condition [reverent obedience] of that approving love, thereby showing it to be a love based upon wisdom, the *Holy Spirit*. This Spirit, through which the love of God as the bestower of beatitude (really our own responding love proportioned to his) is combined with the fear of God as Lawgiver, i.e., the conditioned with the condition, which thus can be represented as "proceeding from both," not only "leads into all truth" (obedience to duty) but is also the real Judge of men (before their own conscience). (*Rel*, p. 136 and n.; *AA*, VI, 145 and n.; translation mine)[12]

Thus everything—radical evil, conversion, justification, election—falls back in the end to a playing out of the primordial confrontation between human freedom and the divine call. Nothing fundamentally new is added from God's side to change the situation. The reason for Kant's reserve is that he was preoccupied with the infinitely high and distant ideal of holiness, and he did not see how the gulf created by finitude and sin could be bridged except forensically, in the mode of imputation and judgment alone, on the basis of man's commitment to the ideal and his steadfast struggle against the evil principle within him. Thus Kant's theology, and any Christology that follows from it, are dominated by the "first article"; and he himself remains a spiritual

---

12. Cf. *Reflexionen*, 6307, *AA*, XVIII, 598–600, where Kant's first and most spontaneous reflections along this line, probably from the early 1780s, can be found among the comments he made in a handwritten copy of some lectures on natural theology by Eberhard of Halle.

child of Abraham, justified by faith and hope, unable to find a settled home in the land of promise.

Yet what Kant has done is useful, precisely because of his reserve, because it indicates—as though we did not know it in any other way!—how there might be a valid relationship with God even prior to or apart from the historical movement and the institutional life known as Christianity. Kant's way of thinking was not lost from sight. It endured, and was even developed further in Schelling during the next generation, and through Schelling it affected the thought of an even later generation in Baur and Strauss. We must take note of him, then, in a kind of appendix to this section.

Schelling did not have the same problem as Kant, for whom the ideal hovers out of reach above human life. Schelling rather felt an embarrassment of riches. He argued, most notably in his *Vorlesungen über die Methode des akademischen Studiums* in 1803 (the eighth and ninth lectures), that Christianity is not a unique and special work of divine providence, for the incarnation of God has been from eternity, in the entire development of the cosmos, and it cannot be exhausted in a single event. Therefore attention must be shifted, he suggested, from the "exoteric" and literal teachings of Christianity to its "esoteric" meaning, uncovered by speculation; and it comes to this:

> The eternal Son of God, begotten from the essence of the Father of all things, is simply the finite itself as it is in God's eternal sight, which appears to be a suffering God subordinated to the misfortunes of time, but at the climax of its manifestation, in Christ, brings to a close the world of finitude and opens up the world of infinitude, the rule of the Spirit. (*SW*, V, 294)

Schelling has a certain importance to the history of modern theology because he reasserted what is really a venerable patristic theme, that the grace of God is operative everywhere and that one would expect to find traces of it among non-Christian cultures even though its complete and accurate expression is found only in the biblical tradition. His way of putting it may be needlessly provocative:

> The Christian missionaries who came to India thought that they would be preaching something unheard of to the inhabitants when they taught that the God of the Christians became man. But they were not surprised by it, they did not dispute the incarnation of God in Christ in

any way; they only found it strange that what had happened among them frequently and with constant repetition had happened among the Christians only once. It cannot be denied that they had gained a better understanding of their religion than the Christian missionaries of theirs. (*SW*, V, 298–99)

However that may be, it struck a note that had many reverberations. We shall have occasion at a later point to suggest what is the place of such a "Christology of the first article," stressing the universal presence of the gracious God within the total pattern of Christian theology.

2. Schleiermacher and the "Second Adam"

If Kant showed the possibility of a Christianity and a Christology without Christ, Schleiermacher, by contrast, took an approach which was strictly delimited to a Christian experience that is always directed toward and dependent upon Christ. His theory of religion stresses, it is well known, subjectivity and feeling. But that theory will be misunderstood if it is forgotten that the religious feeling to which he refers is not raw, generally accessible experience, but experience which has already been evoked and shaped by linguistic and liturgical and doctrinal traditions, producing a distinct and definite mind-set, a patterning of attitudes and assumptions and emotional tones. In all of this the primacy belongs, as one might expect, to liturgy and hymnody before the rhetoric of preaching, and certainly before the didacticism of theology. When Schleiermacher explicates the Christian consciousness, as he does in his *Glaubenslehre*, he does not rely on anything that might be supposed to be common to the Christian and the non-Christian; what he treasures is that which belongs to the central experiences of the Christian. Although he, in common with others of his age, will try to reduce to a minimum the element of arbitrary "positivity" and external authority, it will be for the purpose of bringing out all the more clearly the frame of mind developed by the tradition of Christian worship and teaching, speaking from faith to faith. He focuses, then, upon the particular, not the general, and upon the actual, not the ideal; for what is most attractive to him about the Christian message is that a style of life which had been a possibility elsewhere, but *only* a possibility, has here become actual. He stays by the actuality, therefore, and does not let his glance stray too far from it, since everything revolves around the Christian experience of sin and redemption.

The work that set the pattern for Schleiermacher's mature position was a long treatise on the doctrine of election, called forth by the debates between the Lutheran and the Reformed factions during the early years of the Prussian Union of 1817.[13] Schleiermacher, a Reformed theologian, set out to defend the Calvinist position on predestination against what he considered ill-advised attacks from the Lutherans, specifically from Bretschneider. He begins with an analysis and presentation of Calvin's *Institutes*, impressive in its ability to get to the central religious concerns and to avoid dealing with it as impersonal theorizing. He lays his groundwork by pointing to the characteristic Reformation doctrines that the Spirit comes to the elect through the hearing of the Word and that the confidence of the elect is always based upon the saving purpose of God, and he keeps the entire discussion within those terms. Then he interprets those Reformation themes in an authentically Calvinist direction.

Schleiermacher praises Calvin for refusing to acknowledge a distinction between God's directly willing the salvation of the elect and his merely permitting the damnation of the reprobate. If permission is not to mean that some things escape God's rule or limit him against his will (and this would be "Manichaeism"), then it must be nothing other than God's "willing not to prevent" an occurrence, and hence it falls within the scope of his ordering and willing (*SW*, I.2, 447). So if the anti-Pelagian side of the Christian consciousness is that there cannot be a pure and joyful attitude toward any good thing except as it is seen as a *gift of God* given for Christ's sake, and to ascribe anything to oneself is felt to be a compromising of one's communion with God, the anti-Manichaean side, just as essential, is that there can be no pure and joyful sense for God's power unless *everything* is referred to him, and insofar as any exceptions are made one feels himself drawn into the sphere of a will and a community opposed to God (p. 449). In good Calvinist fashion, then, Schleiermacher ascribes all the vicissitudes of man's religious consciousness to the one and undivided counsel or decree of God.

But we must note the pattern emerging from these predestinarian statements. Schleiermacher points out that even the Calvinists see the

---

13. "Ueber die Lehre von der Erwählung, besonders in Beziehung auf Herrn Dr. Bretschneiders Aphorismen," *Sämmtliche Werke*, I.2 (Berlin: G. Reimer, 1836), 393–484 (first published in *Theologische Zeitschrift*, I [1819]: 1–119).

act of redemption in Christ, and the Word that communicates it, as universal in their potency—although they also insist that some men fail to believe because God did not will that they believe (pp. 429–40). But when they fail to believe, it is still they who are to blame, not God, since the impulses of the Spirit, coming through the Word, are of infinite power, while their own desires to resist are only finite. What makes the difference, then, between those who respond and those who do not is that there is either a favorable or an unfavorable combination of inducements offered, on one side from the Word and on the other from the temptations of the flesh (pp. 406–9). This is not surprising, and it is not arbitrary, for each individual is who he is within his own concrete situation and in the midst of all those relationships that affect his unfolding of himself, and the sum of them is the entire historical process, ordered by God himself. Thus election does not take place with a separate decree for each person; it envisages the whole, and each individual has a well-defined place within it.

This begins to look like an unremitting determinism. The point, however, is simply that spiritual rebirth occurs, according to God's own wisdom, in a way analogous to natural birth, through contagion and growth when the conditions are right, when there is receptivity to the Word and Spirit. What constitutes that receptivity is not a set of natural circumstances, mechanistically determined, but something spiritual, within the heart of man—*the sense of sin and guilt.* Christ indicated the conditions of the Spirit's operation when he said that he came to call sinners to repentance, those who need a physician; in other words, his call, issued on all sides, operates with the greatest force upon those who feel sin most strongly. Therefore when the Calvinists say that in some sense even the fall of man into sin lies within God's counsel, they mean not that man was fated to sin but that God willed to bring man to fulfillment *through awareness of his need and dependence upon redemption,* willed, in other words, to bring the first creation to its completion along the way that leads through repentance and a new creation (pp. 451–52). God is *not* the author of sin if by this it is meant that he directly causes it; and yet "apart from the law sin lies dead" (Romans 7:8)—the *sense* of sin and damnation *is* aroused by the divine presence, wounding man in order to heal him, and not healing him except where he has first been wounded.

Thus final and efficient causes coincide: when Paul says in Romans

9–11 that the Word has operated upon Gentiles more powerfully than upon Jews, it first appears to be a teleological statement that the fullness of the Gentiles must enter into the kingdom in order that all of Israel gain it; but what is really meant is that the Jews think themselves healthy, and only the healing of the Gentiles will lead the Jews to feel their sickness (p. 473). So the definiteness of the instant of conversion, which seems to be either arbitrary or coincidental, is based upon man's intrinsic receptivity to divine influence, and everything takes place in a way analogous to natural growth, with the awareness of need coming first and preparing the way for a joyful reception of new life in the Spirit through trust in the Word of redemption. The decree of election and rejection means, descriptively, that those who hear the Word and are given life, according to their readiness at a particular time and place, are the elect; the others are the reprobate. The election and rejection of individuals is, however, only one aspect of the *single eternal decree* by which God wills, in unqualified love, to build the human race into the body of Christ in a "natural" way. For God's good pleasure is related, in the last analysis, not to isolated individuals but to a *world*, and the Spirit operates through the Word as a power creating a new spiritual world (pp. 474–76).

Furthermore, Schleiermacher discloses at the end that he has been speaking only about the observable historical sequence in which people receive the gospel, not about eternal salvation and damnation. In connection with this latter theme he concedes that the rejection of some—or rather, all—of the human race is a necessary correlate of divine justice. But if it is a necessity, he adds, it is a necessity only as a *stage of development*, and therefore "even the damned cannot be excluded from being the objects of divine love, for *everything* that belongs to the well-ordered world of living beings must be the object of *all* the divine attributes" (p. 479). The difference between nonbelievers and believers, the reprobate and the elect, is only a difference between *earlier* and *later* reception into the kingdom of Christ, a difference which follows quite naturally from the temporality of human life and God's decree that his grace is to be received only by those who know their need. The point still holds, nevertheless, that no person is saved without first becoming aware of his lostness. Everything must be said in terms of sin and redemption.

All of this helps us to approach Schleiermacher's dogmatic work, *The*

Christian Faith, with a sense for the proportion among its parts. It really should be begun half way through, with the discussion of the "antithesis between sin and grace," for the discussion of the religious self-consciousness in general, which precedes it, belongs to the work only insofar as this general consciousness is presupposed by and contained in the Christian consciousness of sin and grace. The introduction to the work as a whole, furthermore, consists merely of *Lehnsätze*, supporting propositions borrowed from disciplines *other* than theology and serving only to characterize Christianity by contrasting it with other phenomena in human life. The content of dogmatics, then, is exhausted by the antithesis and whatever it presupposes or takes into itself. It is necessary to omit from direct consideration everything that is prior to Christianity, as well as the eschatological resolution of the antithesis for which the Christian himself hopes (*Gl*, § 29, 3).[14]

In *The Christian Faith* he asserts even more clearly than in the essay on election that sin is grounded in human freedom and is not caused by God: it is a failure to keep the God-consciousness supreme over other impulses, a stunting of the well-ordered spiritual growth that might have been achieved. Yet the blunt fact is that in the development of each individual the satisfaction of desire has come *well before* the rise of any moral and religious consciousness. If so, it would seem that man cannot be held culpable for his sin, since he did not enter upon it knowingly or voluntarily, from a situation of indeterminacy. This, it will be recalled, is the same kind of restatement of the doctrine of original sin that we have seen in Kant; it also has the same perplexities, which will receive the same resolution. For Schleiermacher, like Kant, thinks that the responsibility and thus the guilt of man is *structural*, following from the fact that, on the one hand, man has a "predisposition" toward a joyous and triumphant cultivation of his God-con-

---

14. For Schleiermacher's difficulties over the arrangement of the work, and his reasons for giving it what he felt to be a misleading order, see the first letter to Lücke (*SW*, I.2, 605–15), and the discussion in Richard R. Niebuhr, *Schleiermacher on Christ and Religion: A New Introduction* (New York: Charles Scribner's & Sons, 1964), pp. 238–43. It should be noted that this conception of the essence of Christianity goes as far back as the first edition of the *Speeches on Religion* in 1799, where he describes it as an "intuition of the universal resistance of finite things to the unity of the Whole, and of the way the Deity treats this resistance" (*On Religion: Speeches to Its Cultured Despisers*, trans. John Oman [London: Routledge & Kegan Paul, 1893; reprinted Harper Torchbooks, 1958], p. 241), and goes on to suggest that the tension between universal corruption and an infinite striving after holiness is resolved only by following the path of redemption (ibid., pp. 243, 246).

sciousness, and, on the other, that there is a gap, indeed, a contradiction, between what he is and what he could have become. In a sense there is, perhaps, an inexorable operation of fate, for all of this follows from the weakness of human life and its inability to develop otherwise than by slow, painful degrees. But the Christian consciousness views this fatality as something accepted by God, or rather as something willed by him as an integral feature of the world because he knows how to put it to good use, making it contribute first to man's awareness of his responsibility and guilt and bondage, then to his redemption.

The center of Schleiermacher's theology is therefore the experience of redemption, the deliverance of the religious consciousness from its bondage to sin and the establishing of its predominance in man's inward life. But here he confronts a puzzle. All that is given with immediate certitude is the Christian's experience of being redeemed; nothing is learned of the actual character of the Redeemer. But of course theology must make some assertions about precisely this. If one wishes to say that Christ is the "second Adam," the realization of the archetypal ideal of humanity (as Schleiermacher did), then the question is whether such an assertion can be made solely on the basis of the Christian's own experience of sin and redemption.[15] In the first edition of *Die christliche Glaube* he acknowledged the difficulty and said that the concept of Christ as second Adam, as fulfiller of creation, is only *"erlaüternd und kombinatorisch"* (Gl^1, § 110, 1), tying together what must be said about "sin as such" and "redemption as such." But he still wanted to assert that Christ is the realization of the archetype (Gl^1 § 110), and that his archetypal perfection is manifested as something unconditioned by time and history, even though it unfolds in time (Gl^1, § 115).

He was challenged on this by F. C. Baur in his inaugural dissertation as a professor at Tübingen in 1827, circulated in German in the form of a summary in the first issue of the *Tübinger Zeitschrift für Theologie* in 1828.[16] Baur criticized the *Glaubenslehre* (the first edition of 1821–22,

---

15. For what follows, see Hans Scheel, *Die Theorie von Christus als dem zweiten Adam bei Schleiermacher* (Leipzig: Deichert, 1913), pp. 53 ff.
16. "Anzeige der beiden academischen Schriften von Dr. F. C. Baur: Primae Rationalismi et Supranaturalismi historiae capita potiora. Pars I. De Gnosticorum Christianismo ideali. Pars. II. Comparatur Gnosticismus cum Schleiermacherianae theologiae indole. Tub. 1827," *Tübinger Zeitschrift für Theologie*, I (1828): 220–64. I am grateful to Prof. Peter C. Hodgson for making available his notes on this

of course) for its failure to make good its claim to unite the "archetypal" and the "historical" in Christ, and he pointed out the parallel with the Gnosticism of the early centuries. Now since Baur is known chiefly as a historian, it would be easy to suppose that he was urging Schleiermacher to make better use of historical evidence in the assertions he made about Christ. To a certain extent this is true, for Baur did reject the kind of "ideal rationalism," as he called it, which claimed to dispense with the historical altogether and favored a second kind of rationalism, one which acknowledges the contribution of the historical to the discovery and formulation of ideas which then can be seen to be fully rational. But the force of the criticisms is quite different from this, although it is well concealed. Baur was unable to see how the ideal archetype could ever be adequately expressed in a finite individual; indeed, he thought that this would violate its ideal character. This is an argument that Baur had learned from Schelling as early as 1818, as his biographer Zeller noted long ago.[17] In a letter written to his brother in 1823, giving his reactions on reading the first edition of Schleiermacher's work, he indicates how it liberated him from the old struggles that had been taking place among the theologians in Tübingen and pointed the way toward a different kind of theology, more congenial to him. But Baur was already looking well beyond his new mentor. What he reacted to most enthusiastically was what he called the "idealist" element in Schleiermacher, his stress on the priority of the religious consciousness, and he was dismayed at what seemed to be Schleiermacher's lapses in the direction of the historical and the authoritarian. His own convictions are already clear, and they are those that will hold throughout his career:

> Thus Christ is in each man, and the outward appearance of Jesus is not even in this case [in the case of Christian belief] what is originative;

---

article. For recent discussions throwing much-needed light on Baur's development, see Heinz Liebing, "Ferdinand Christian Baurs Kritik an Schleiermachers Glaubenslehre," *Zeitschrift für Theologie und Kirche*, LIV (1957): 225–43; Wolfgang Geiger, *Spekulation und Kritik. Die Geschichtstheologie Ferdinand Christian Baurs* (Munich: Chr. Kaiser, 1964); Peter C. Hodgson, *The Formation of Historical Theology: A Study of Ferdinand Christian Baur* (New York: Harper & Row, 1966); Gotthold Müller, *Identität und Immanenz. Zur Genese der Theologie von David Friedrich Strauss. Eine theologie- und philosophiegeschichtliche Studie* (Zurich: EVZ, 1968).
17. Müller, pp. 180–95, 219–22.

but rather the archetypal, the ideal, ought to be traced in the historical and the inner consciousness be brought to clear intuition.[18]

Let us note exactly what it was that Baur was doing, and for this the readiest source is his work on *Die christliche Gnosis*, published in 1835 after many years of study and reflection. He thought of Gnosticism as not merely a movement in the early centuries but an enduring type of Christian thought, a "philosophy of religion" which began from the historical and ascended to the ideal, of which the historical is merely a manifestation. Obviously this tendency in ancient Christianity, given an orthodox form in Clement of Alexandria, had its counterpart in recent German philosophy; and Baur intended to point out the parallels and defend this type of thinking as the most promising course for theology.

When he comes to Schleiermacher (*Gnosis*, pp. 637–68) his argument is that the actual character of the *Glaubenslehre*, despite a sincere attempt to hold the archetypal and the historical together, is Gnostic: the two cannot be brought together in perfect unity but drift apart, just as the Gnostics, in their less sophisticated and more imaginative way, found that "Christ" and "Jesus," or the spiritual and the material, drift apart; and the former, of course, is what must be given precedence. Schleiermacher, he thinks, is really engaged in "philosophy of religion" despite his protestations, and Baur's proof is the assertion that all dogmatic propositions can be reduced to what Schleiermacher calls the "first form," that which describes modes of the religious self-consciousness.[19] Baur thinks that he has got "a deeper glimpse of the inmost structure" of the *Glaubenslehre* (*Gnosis*, p. 652), and the insight is that religious feeling develops itself out of its own resources by a coherent dialectic.

---

18. Liebing, pp. 242–43. Cf. his own observations on Baur's difficulties with Schleiermacher's Christology, pp. 234–37.

19. See the two long discursive footnotes, pp. 646–52, where he argues that this is the character of the introduction to *Die christliche Glaube* and rejects the move made by Schleiermacher in the second edition to separate the *Lehnsätze* of the introduction from the body of his dogmatics. The introduction is either a part of the dogmatics, or it is superfluous, he argues; and since the introduction deals with many things of substantive importance (especially the notion of redemption) it must be taken as an indication of the way Schleiermacher was actually thinking about dogmatic matters.

Even the whole doctrine of the person of Christ is therefore nothing else, finally, than the description of a human state, namely, that of redemption, and the Redeemer is nothing else than the Idea of redemption, considered under personal form in him and permanently fixed to his person. Into the place of the historical Christ steps the ideal or archetypal Christ, in whom the perfect God-consciousness on which redemption is conditioned is represented as a "being," and human God-consciousness becomes a being of God in human nature. (*Gnosis,* p. 652)

Baur thinks he can show that Schleiermacher's Christology is in all essentials the same as that sketched by Kant in his *Religion* (*Gnosis,* pp. 660–68):

That about which Kant leaves us in no doubt, that the Redeemer as the man pleasing to God, the ideal of a humanity pleasing to God, is only a personification of the good principle in its absolute victory over the evil, is also the real significance of Schleiermacher's archetypal Christ. The archetypal Christ, the God-man, the absolutely sinless and perfect man, is nothing else than the personalized idea of redemption, redemption itself insofar as it is thought of, however, as realized in an individual, the God-consciousness in its absolute constancy and power, to which the God-consciousness of the individuals who make up the Christian community merely stand in a relation of constant approximation. (*Gnosis,* p. 664)

In both thinkers the individual is united to the "Redeemer" through a change of disposition, and this is sufficient for justification, despite the remnants of sin. In other words, to adopt the good principle into one's disposition is to have the Redeemer within oneself. The only difference between them is that Kant knew very well the limits of external manifestation and preferred from the outset to rest his case on pure practical reason, while Schleiermacher, operating as a theologian within the community in which the idea of redemption was first brought to consciousness, wants to make Jesus an adequate and unequaled actualization of the idea. And yet this means nothing more than that a power of God-consciousness which is really "natural," within the range of man's potentialities, is experienced as "supernatural" because it is actuated from beyond oneself, by the influence emanating from Jesus of Nazareth.

We should note that there is one aspect of Schleiermacher's thought which makes him susceptible to this line of interpretation. In his early dialogue *Christmas Eve* (1805) the influence of Schelling is apparent.[20] The setting is a family, and the first theme to be struck—and it also dominates the ending, after frequent appearances along the way—is that every mother is another Mary who sees the stirrings of the divine within her child, so that Christmas is primarily a celebration of the power of God at work everywhere in human life. The true "Son of God" is said to be humanity as such, the idea of humanity in the original creative power of God—although it is also acknowledged that men are separated from the eternal and become aware of their own potential for a new, untrammeled life only through the influence of one who did not have to overcome this cleavage but was "man as such" from birth.

Indeed, Schleiermacher held to this way of thinking throughout his career. For him the "idea" of humanity is always to be found in the original self-impartation of God in the creation of human nature with all its potentialities, and the "miraculous" character of Jesus, like that of all other "heroes" in human history, consists quite simply in the eruption of something new into the common life of men out of this universal fountain of life (*Gl*, §§ 13, 1; 93, 3). Even in the final edition of the *Glaubenslehre* he discusses Christ under a section devoted to the "first form" of dogmatic proposition, thus as one instance of human religious consciousness as the perfect actualization of what all are in potentiality. Yet, in spite of everything, the focus of Schleiermacher's theology is *not* upon this underlying identity of human potential but upon the dependence of all believers on the real historic person of Jesus, a dependence which is so fundamental that the self-impartation of God is refracted into three irreducible modes.

That Schleiermacher took Baur's criticisms seriously is shown by the frequent mention made of them in the two "letters to Lücke" published in *Theologische Studien und Kritiken*, the organ of Schleiermacher's

---

20. On the often controversial interpretation of this dialogue see especially Karl Barth, "Schleiermacher's *Celebration of Christmas*," *Theology and Church: Shorter Writings, 1920–1928*, trans. Louise Pettibone Smith (London: SCM Press, 1962), pp. 136–58; Richard R. Niebuhr, *Schleiermacher on Christ and Religion: A New Introduction* (London: SCM Press, 1962), pp. 21–71; Terence N. Tice, Introduction to his translation of *Christmas Eve* (Richmond: John Knox, 1967); and Emanuel Hirsch, "Schleiermachers 'Weihnachtsfeier,'" *Schleiermachers Christusglaube. Drei Studien* (Gütersloh: Gerd Mohn, 1968), pp. 7–52.

followers, in 1829. He thinks Baur has misunderstood his method, he says, chiefly because of his statement that the "first form of dogmatic proposition" is the essential one. His reply is that this is purely a matter of logical form and systematic structure, not of content. If a theology can do without statements about historical occurrences, this does not mean that it has no historical foundation at all, no real Christ as the object of its faith. His point had been only that the other two forms of statement can contain nothing more than what is implied or presupposed by the first form (*SW*, I.2, 627–29, 636–37). Nevertheless he does acknowledge that he had been thinking too narrowly about redemption. The fifteenth question of the Heidelberg Catechism had been so appealing to him, he says, as an immediate expression of Christian feeling, that he neglected to inquire any further. That question, to be sure, has an "ideal Christ," for it asks, "What sort of Mediator and Redeemer must we then seek?" But it also assumes that this ideal Christ is historical, for the answer is, "For one who is very man, and perfectly righteous, and yet more powerful than all creatures, that is, one who is also very God." He will have to take this problem into account in the second edition of the *Glaubenslehre*, he says (*SW*, I.2, 624–25).

In the first edition the stress had been, in good Reformation fashion, on the sense of guilt and incapacity, man's inability to effect a change in his life and his subsequent relation of dependence and trust toward Christ as Redeemer. The *fact* of conversion was taken as evidence of its *cause*, for the only adequate explanation for the conversion of sinful man is an already existing life of sinless perfection which somehow effects it. This is the essential feature of Schleiermacher's theology, what makes it always a "theology of the second article."

In the second edition none of this was lost. He argued, against Baur, that the ideal for humanity will remain ineffectual, "a bare possibility," and man's potentialities will remain unfulfilled until the ideal becomes perfectly actualized somewhere:

> it may be said of all more limited kinds of being that their concept is perfectly realized in the totality of individuals, which complete each other. But this cannot hold of a species which develops itself freely, if the perfection of an essential vital function be posited in the concept but actually found in no individual; for perfection cannot be obtained by adding together things that are imperfect. (*Gl*, § 93, 2)

Because man is free, responsible for actualizing himself, he can also come under bondage, and a mere ideal is powerless to release his potentialities. But what of Baur's suggestion that the feeling of trust in another as Redeemer is merely a projection on the part of believers, contemplating the ideal in the mirror of their own imperfection? Schleiermacher must attempt to explain the nature of the influence emanating from Christ. He does it by describing redemption as a process of being drawn into the power of Christ's own God-consciousness, on the basis of which the believer is then able to say something about the inner life of Christ.

Schleiermacher takes pains to give a clear account of this incorporation into the power of Christ's God-consciousness (*Gl*, §§ 100–1). It is, he says, a "mystical" mode of influence and participation, by which he means that a life common to Christ and believers is established through preaching, the sacraments, and other forms of communication. The priority of Christ and the unceasing dependence of others upon his perfection can be established from the very character of the experience, he thinks, for one knows oneself to be challenged and attracted to a higher mode of life by the Redeemer himself or by what is said about him, and thus any inclination within oneself toward that mode of life is felt to be "his act become ours," "Christ in us" (*Gl*, § 100, 1).[21] In this way Schleiermacher is able to affirm what was an embarrassment to most thinkers of his era, an influence of Christ that grows in a natural way, through spatio-temporal means, in the history of a particular religion; but it is to be noted that he could affirm it only because he thought primarily in terms of words and symbols, operating in the quite special atmosphere of human consciousness.

Assuming that this account is at least plausible on the side of the *subject*, let us see what Schleiermacher is able to affirm about *Jesus*, and ask especially whether he is able to escape the accusation of making him a mere projection of one's own awareness of the ideal. If Christ can be Redeemer only because he is in reality the Fulfiller, the actualization of the archetypal ideal (*Gl*, § 89), then it is difficult to

---

21. Cf. the discussion in the *Speeches* of the "holy sadness" which is the "ground tone" of Christian feeling, a mixture of pride and humility (*On Religion*, p. 245), which Schleiermacher describes in his notes added in the later editions (*On Religion*, pp. 262–63) as humility in what one is "over against Christ" and pride in what one is "in fellowship with Christ" and with "the acquisition of all Christ's perfections"—a pride, as we may presume, which is compatible with a feeling of total dependence.

understand how such a perfectly sinless being could even be relevant to a sinful humanity. He would seem so unlike them that they would find nothing in common between themselves and him, and he would remain a foreign body within human history. Especially because Schleiermacher describes the religious self-consciousness as a constant, self-identical feature of human life and calls the sinlessness of Christ a "miraculous" eruption of this innate feeling from within, he has often been accused of making Christ's archetypal perfection an inert state *before* and *behind* any interactions with the surrounding world or with other persons, insulated from harm or temptation. If so, he would be open to the charge that his Christology was excessively deductive in method and Docetist in substance.[22] How can one speak of perfection being actualized in the midst of a sinful humanity without its seeming implausible, or, if not implausible, then irrelevant? This is a problem far more central to Schleiermacher's theology than the logical problem, dear to the followers of Schelling and Hegel, concerning the relation of the archetypal to the historical; or rather, it is the proper way of phrasing this latter problem within the framework of Schleiermacher's own thought.

I think that Schleiermacher had a better answer than these criticisms would suggest. Although it is true that for him the victorious God-consciousness of Jesus develops from within, out of the creative sources of human life, it is never out of contact with those influences that are all too familiar in the life of man. One of Schleiermacher's central principles is that God-consciousness develops only in response to external stimuli and in relation to real situations (*Gl*, § 5, 3–4); and this holds true in the case of Christ as well. Although in him God-consciousness always predominated over sensuous consciousness, it developed only to the extent that the latter developed, and thus sinlessness is compatible with genuine growth from innocence to experience (*Gl*, § 93, 4). Schleiermacher knew, too, that Christ must have shared in the same vicissitudes and temptations, the same influences from sinful society, as the others (*Gl*, § 94, 1). All of this, indeed, is essential to what

22. This is one of Baur's chief difficulties with Schleiermacher, brought out explicitly in *DM*, p. 966; it is also found in a writing by Hegel's chief theological representative during the generation after his death, Karl Rosenkranz's *Kritik der Schleiermacherschen Glaubenslehre* (Königsberg, 1836). pp. 76–77, 80–81; and it is a major theme in Hans Scheel's *Die Theorie von Christus als dem Zweiten Adam bei Schleiermacher*, esp. pp. 66–67.

Schleiermacher asserted about Christ's highest dignity, that there is a "being of God in him." We can speak only of God's being "in" the world as a whole, Schleiermacher thought, not of his being in individual things, for God is pure activity and individual things are enmeshed in the reciprocal activities and passivities that constitute the whole. When human consciousness opens itself without restriction toward the whole, not passively but with "vital receptivity" (teleologically, having a sense for the further tasks of interpreting and shaping the whole in accordance with the love of God), and with a clearly focused and triumphant God-consciousness in every moment, then it can be said that God is "in" Christ (§§ 94, 2; 96, 3). His archetypal purity, therefore, is achieved not in isolation from the turmoil of the world but in active commerce with it, and his perfection is manifested in its most convincing fullness when it overcomes even opposition, suffering, and death (§ 101, 4). Even the element of incompleteness and striving which is the keynote of Schleiermacher's understanding of Christian ethics is ascribed to Christ himself, though with respect not to his God-consciousness but to his taking the problems of others upon himself: "the deficiency in him consists in his broadened self-consciousness, in his sympathy with our misery, and it is for him the impulse toward his whole redeeming activity" (*Die christliche Sitte*, SW, I. 12, 39).

Yet, despite statements like these which give recognition to a close relationship between Christ and the human condition, there are several aspects of Schleiermacher's Christology which remain "Docetist" in tendency. One is an inability to come to terms with the particularities of Jesus' life and surroundings and a tendency rather to look past them, as being a matter of indifference, to his inward life, his "God-consciousness." The reason is Schleiermacher's desire to exhibit Jesus' archetypal characteristics more clearly and to make him relevant to all peoples, without any closer ties to some (even to Israel!) than to others. This attempt is legitimate, of course, to the extent that inward life does transcend external influences and may not be fully expressed in the patterns of language and action that are available in a culture (*Gl*, § 93, 2–5). The other is Schleiermacher's denial that Jesus could really be tempted, for this seems to him to be already a tending toward sin. Pleasure and pain belong to human life, he knows, but they must be experienced, he insists, without leading to temptation. The New

Testament narratives and assertions that speak of temptations are simply dismissed as historically questionable and religiously irrelevant (*Gl*, § 98). These are convincing examples of Schleiermacher's tendency toward wishful or deductive thinking, what Baur characterized as "Gnosticism." By themselves, however, they would be evidence only of a residual pietism or of naiveté about historical method, not of a fundamental defect in the pattern of Schleiermacher's theology.

But we also find, unfortunately, a defect even in the overarching theological pattern. Although Schleiermacher's first impulse, as we have seen, was to say that God willed to impart his gracious presence to men only in the mode of redemption, after they had become aware of their guilt and inability, so that they would share in the peace of a new life only by way of contrast with its opposite, he spoiled that insight in his speculations about the place of Christ within the divine economy, under a single eternal decree (*Gl*, §§ 86–89, 164–69). The fundamental reason for this, I suspect, is his adoption of a modalist conception of the Trinity, according to which the sole meaning of the doctrine is that God imparts himself to humanity in three different ways, first in human nature, then in Christ, and finally in the common spirit of the Christian community—in other words, that God eternally wills a gradual development of human nature, reaching its perfection only in Christ and in the dependence of others upon him. This enabled him to prove deductively that Jesus is the actualization of the archetypal ideal, since the creation of mankind reaches completion only in him; he is, in the strongest possible sense, the Second Adam, the new creation (*Gl*, §§ 89, 164). But in the process Schleiermacher had to go beyond the immediate religious consciousness that grace comes only to those who are aware of their sin, and adopt the speculative doctrine of both Calvin and Spinoza that it *must* happen in this way since alternative possibilities are totally unreal and all events are locked into a single network of relationships decreed by God (*Gl*, § 89, 3). He had to go beyond the immediate religious consciousness of Jesus as Redeemer and adopt the speculative doctrine that he is Redeemer only because he is first the Fulfiller of creation, emerging miraculously from innocence into spiritual perfection (*Gl*, § 93, 4). One can only conclude that, if it is necessary to develop speculative overbeliefs such as these in order to maintain a modalist doctrine of the Trinity, then it is preferable to keep the traditional distinction between the eternal Trinity and the "missions" of the Son and the Spirit, whose purpose is to repair the damage done by the free and contingent fact of sin.

It would have been better, both for the consistency of Schleiermacher's theology and for the credibility of his picture of Jesus, if he had given a redemptive purpose to the very presence of Christ, if he had described the development of his "God-consciousness" as taking place not in isolation, "outside" the corporate life of sin (*Gl*, § 88, 4), but rather *within* and *against* it—if he had said, not that Jesus is Redeemer because he is Fulfiller, but rather that he is Fulfiller precisely as Redeemer.[23] For the chief virtue of Schleiermacher's theology is that he constructed a framework of christological thinking which could describe Jesus in human terms without giving up the "archetypal" aspects that are implied in what has been asserted about him. He could do this because he conceived the ideal of humanity "teleologically," that is, as the subordinating of all man's powers and all his finite relationships to the consciousness of God. Thus it is not an empty ideal or one that will always hover above human life. It can be given reality, and it *must* be given reality, for only then will its power be felt. Schleiermacher's sustaining conviction was that both sides—the ideal and the real—come together harmoniously in the Christian message about Christ, and he tried, in addition, to bring all his statements into relation with the believer's experience of redemption. The intention should be honored despite its flawed realization.

I have suggested that Schleiermacher's is a "Christology of the second article" because of its intense concentration upon sin and

23. Paul Tillich continues and corrects Schleiermacher's Christology in this respect. He takes the archetype Christology quite seriously, but he makes the problem of sin (existential estrangement) integral to everything he says about Jesus as the actualization of essential humanity. For him the Church's proclamation of "Jesus as the Christ" means that "he represents the original image of God embodied in man, but he does so under the conditions of estrangement between God and man"—that "in one personal life essential manhood has appeared under the conditions of existence without being conquered by them" (*Systematic Theology*, II [Chicago: University of Chicago Press, 1957], 94; cf. 98, 114, 119–35, 150–65). Jesus becomes and remains the Christ *only as finite freedom*, confronting the real temptations, limitations, and tragic conflicts of earthly life, even opposition and suffering and death, and overcoming them only as he makes them a part of his union with God (II, 125–35).

Even stronger (although it is not in the line of succession from Schleiermacher) is the tradition leading from Gottfried Menken and Edward Irving to J. C. K. von Hofmann, H. F. Kohlbrügge, Eduard Böhl, and Hermann Bezzel, which holds that Christ assumed "sinful flesh"—that is, the full human condition, with its active inclinations toward sin—and overcame its temptations in the power of the Holy Spirit (cf. *CD*, I/2, 153–55; Otto Weber, *Grundlagen der Dogmatik*, II [Neukirchen: Kreis Moers, 1962], 162).

redemption. In this he is one of the most authentic followers of Paul that we will find among modern theologians. The implications become especially clear in his understanding of the life of the Christian community. It is, he says, an extension or an image of the work of Christ, and it is a "being of God" within human life, just as in him—but in a different mode. God has imparted himself first in the creation and sustaining of human nature with all its hidden resources for development; then in a different way in Christ as the fulfillment of those powers in a "person-forming" union with God; then in another way again in the "common spirit" of the community arising from Christ, working "in and "through" its members, exerting influence on behalf of Christ in the absence of his direct personal influence (*Gl*, §§ 116, 3; 122, 3; 123, 2; 125, 1). This time it is not a person-forming union: a new life is grafted onto the old, and even though there is constant progress the personal continuity with the "old man" cannot be annihilated. Consequently there is a constant dependence on the influence of Christ as it comes through the message and the ethos of the Church (*Gl*, §§ 121-25).

The life of the Church is thus the experience of the individual Christian writ large—the extending of new life in the Spirit through the influence of the Word, a constant struggle with evil, both individual and communal, never arriving at complete victory, but steadily advancing. This does not mean that the world plan balances precariously upon the perfection of Christ in the middle, with imperfection before and behind. The goal toward which God's self-impartation is directed is the "kingdom of God," and the Church has every right to look expectantly toward that consummation. But very little can be said about it by dogmatics, which must be true to its method and operate only on the basis of the Christian consciousness (*Gl*, §§ 157, 164). While man is still on the way toward that goal, the nature of the power that is at work can be fully attested only by Christian ethics, the expression of Christian feeling in its moments of activity and striving, and no longer by dogmatics, the expression of that same feeling in its moments of completion and rest;

> for we are now confronted with the task of more and more securing recognition that the world is a good world, as also of forming all things into an organ of the divine Spirit in harmony with the divine idea originally underlying the world-order, thus bringing all into unity with the system of redemption. The purpose of this is that in both respects we

may attain to perfect living fellowship with Christ, both insofar as the Father has given him power over all things and insofar as he ever shows him greater works than those he already knows. Hence the world can be viewed as a perfect revelation of divine wisdom only in proportion as the Holy Spirit makes itself felt through the Christian Church as the ultimate world-shaping power. (*Gl*, § 169, 3)

At the University of Berlin another man, the center of a quite different circle of admirers, thought it possible to get somewhat closer to the fulfillment by following another way. Our next task, then, is to look at the theological activities of Georg Wilhelm Friedrich Hegel.

3. Hegel and "Divine-Human Unity"

Hegel's entire intellectual career was, among other things, an attempt to disengage himself from the kind of irrevocable dependence upon Jesus that was so central to Schleiermacher, and, in a different vein, from the sense of distance from the divine ideal that was so important to Kant. Although he acknowledged that both of these approaches had a certain pedagogical value, and even necessity, in human history, his chief concern was to get beyond them. For him, the archetypal idea finally had to be located neither in Kant's realm of abstraction nor in the Jesus continually made present by the Church but in the midst of human life, taking effect in it and shaping it in concrete ways.

He began, we should remind ourselves, as a student of theology in Tübingen during the 1790s, and among his companions were Schelling and Hölderlin. All of them soon breathed the exhilarating influences of that era—Kant's critical philosophy, still being issued in a succession of writings, Herder's pantheism and his interest in the multiplicity of national cultures, the Hellenism of Schiller and Goethe—and they forsook their original calling, moving in divergent directions. Hegel's development during those years has come to light in a number of manuscripts, published under the misleading description of "early theological writings."[24]

24. *Hegels theologische Jugendschriften*, ed. Herman Nohl (Tübingen: J. C. B. Mohr, 1907); the most important of these manuscripts are contained in *On Christianity: Early Theological Writings*, trans. T. M. Knox, with an introduction by Richard Kroner (Chicago: University of Chicago Press, 1948; Harper Torchbooks, 1961). Extensive discussions of them will be found in Wilhelm Dilthey, "Die Jugendgeschichte Hegels," *Gesammelte Schriften*, IV (Leipzig and Berlin. Teubner, 1921), 5–187, and Theodor Haering, *Hegel, sein Wollen und sein Werk. Eine*

It is obvious that Christianity was the chief problem that Hegel had to resolve for himself during those years. He still felt a basic loyalty to the person of Jesus. But he had been persuaded by Lessing and Kant that the only real value of Christianity was the moral religion it conveyed, and in that spirit he wrote a "life of Jesus" (1795) which depicted him as a teacher of a moral faith opposed to the legalism of the Jews, stressing the importance of a virtuous disposition and denying that the ritual observances of "positive" religion could fulfill man's calling.[25] But Hegel had even more basic concerns than this. Herder had shown him the power of national culture, and Schiller and Hölderlin, along with his own reading of the Greek classics, had exhibited to him the communal spirit and the organic unity of Greek culture. The Christian world had obviously failed to produce a folk religion, and in the privacy of his own room he engaged in biting polemic:

> Christianity has emptied Valhalla, felled the sacred groves, extirpated the national imagery as a shameful superstition, as a devilish poison, and given us instead the imagery of a nation whose climate, laws, culture, and interests are strange to us and whose history has no connection whatever with our own. (Knox, p. 146; Nohl, p. 215)

---

chronologische Entwicklungsgeschichte der Gedanken und der Sprache Hegels (Leipzig and Berlin: Teubner, 1929 and 1938). Mention should also be made of Kroner's introduction to the English translation, and what is in part a criticism of it, Walter Kaufmann, "The Young Hegel and Religion," *From Shakespeare to Existentialism: Studies in Poetry, Religion, and Philosophy* (Boston: Beacon Press, 1959), pp. 120–49, as well as Kaufmann's more extensive discussions of the young Hegel in the earlier portions of *Hegel: Reinterpretation, Texts, and Commentary* (New York: Doubleday, 1965). In a richer historical vein there is a study of Hegel's political attitudes by the Marxist Georg Lúkacs in *Der junge Hegel. Ueber die Beziehungen von Dialektik und Oekonomie* (Zurich: Europa Verlag, 1948). Günter Rohrmoser has pointed out, in response to Lúkacs, the religious influences on his thought; see especially "Zur Vorgeschichte der Jugendschriften Hegels," *Zeitschrift für philosophische Forschung*, XIV (1960): 182–208; *Subjektivität und Verdinglichung. Theologie und Gesellschaft im Denken des jungen Hegel* (Gütersloh: Gerd Mohn, 1961); and "Die theologische Bedeutung von Hegels Auseinandersetzung mit der Philosophie Kants und dem Prinzip der Subjektivität," *Neue Zeitschrift für systematische Theologie*, IV (1962): 89–111.

25. Anyone who comes to the writings of this period after a reading of Kant's *Religion within the Limits of Reaason Alone*, just published in 1793 and 1794, will be struck by the absence of any echoes of the most characteristic themes of that work, but he will also have to acknowledge that some of Hegel's ideas could only have come from it. The puzzle is resolved by Haering (pp. 129–30), who shows that Hegel's knowledge of Kant during these years came from reading not the works themselves but discussions of them in the *Neue theologische Journal*. This explains the curious lapses in Hegel's "Kantianism" prior to 1799 or thereabout, when his command of Kant (and his reserve toward him) increases.

It is not that he wanted to revive the old Germanic mythology—that was something he found totally alien to himself. But he was convinced that a religion had to be integrated into the physical surroundings and life patterns of a people. This will always be characteristic of Hegel; it appears later in what he says about the state and culture; and it is rooted in his philosophical principles. For he accepted the negative consequences of Kant's critique of knowledge, that one cannot philosophize about a *transcendent* world. Therefore the ultimate principles must be found *within* the world of life and experience, its relationships, its tensions (even its oppositions), and their resolutions.[26] To say this is not to lapse once more into the "positive," the merely given, that which is arbitrary and based on authority. It means rather that the rational enters into the finite and particular, shaping it to its own ends. He knew this early, and had it fully formulated by 1799:

> The *general concept* of human nature admits of infinite modifications; and there is no need of the makeshift of calling experience to witness that modifications are necessary and that human nature has never been present in its purity . . . . But the *living nature* of man is always other than the concept of the same, and hence what for the concept is a bare modification, a pure accident, a superfluity, becomes a necessity, something living, perhaps the only thing which is natural and beautiful. (Knox, p. 169; Nohl, pp. 140–41; emphasis added)

He is not surprised, therefore, to find religion always linked with particular circumstances and conveyed through sensory images, for he thinks this natural and inevitable:

> imperishability and sacrosanctity may be linked with accidentality, and must be linked with *something* accidental; in thinking of the eternal, we must link the eternal with the accidentality of our own thinking. (Knox, p. 171; Nohl, p. 143)

He has enough confidence in human rationality to feel that religion can never have been pure stupidity or immorality. A religion is not "positive" by the bare fact that sensory media are used in its communication, for these may be the expression of generous insights and feelings

---

26. Cf. Dilthey, "Die Jugendgeschichte Hegels," pp. 154–55 and 180–87, for a somewhat dramatic and overwrought but basically accurate statement of these points as they appear in the early writings.

which are universal in their import; it "becomes positive," and this happens when its imagery and rituals claim too much for themselves:

> the question about positivity does not affect the content of a religion so much as the way in which the religion is conceived, i.e., whether as something given throughout or as something given *qua* free and freely received. (Knox, p. 174; Nohl, p. 144)

Hegel wanted to explain how Christianity had arisen and how it had degenerated into a positive religion. This turns out to be his most fruitful question, and there is a direct continuity between the early fragments entitled by the editor "The Positivity of the Christian Religion" (1795–96) and "The Spirit of Christianity and Its Fate" (1799) and the published writings that deal with the development of Christianity, the *Phenomenology of Spirit* (1807) and the *Lectures on the Philosophy of Religion*, delivered during the 1820s and published after Hegel's death (1832; 1840; critical edition by Lasson, 1929). Although he was not able to create a popular religion, and eventually renounced any such attempt with the observation that the philosopher can only look backward and extract pure concepts out of the figurative thinking of others, he did become a brilliant philosopher of culture whose views dominated much of the work of nineteenth-century historians and whose insights remain impressive even in our own day, when the magic spell surrounding Hegel has dissipated.

He saw from the first that the conquest of the pagan world by Christianity had been prepared by a secret revolution in the spirit of the age, and the explanation he consistently offered was the loss of national autonomy through the Roman conquests, with the Roman people themselves finally losing their freedom like all the others.

> Greek and Roman religion was a religion for free peoples only, and with the loss of freedom its significance and strength, its fitness to men's needs, were also bound to perish. (Knox, p. 154; Nohl, p. 221)

All of the concerns of the individual had been bound up with the life of his city or nation; it was only in moments of leisure or of despair that he had thought at all of his own soul and its destiny. But with the rise of empire and the loss of effective participation in civic life, the individual was uprooted and thrown back upon himself—upon a self

already deprived of an organic cultural life in which he could partici-
pate. Still needing some "idea" that challenged him, some homeland to
which he could belong, he *projected* something to satisfy these needs—
an "objective" God, and a Church whose fulfillment would be in
heaven.

> Thus the despotism of the Roman emperors had chased the human
> spirit from the earth and spread a misery which compelled men to seek
> and expect happiness in heaven; robbed of freedom, their spirit, their
> eternal and absolute element, was forced to take flight to the deity.
> God's objectivity is a counterpart to the corruption and slavery of man,
> and it is strictly only a revelation, only a manifestation of the spirit of
> the age. (Knox, pp. 162–63; Nohl, pp. 227–28)

This analysis of the dynamics of consciousness was carried forward
in the *Phenomenology*, and from there it influenced Feuerbach and
Marx, Nietzsche and Freud, the whole modern critique of religion as
an alienation of man's highest capacities and a projection of them upon
a supposed transcendent being, through whose mediation man then
receives back the power to act (though in other, more dependent and
ineffectual forms) and gains hope for fulfillment and happiness
(though again only in illusory modes). It was a brilliant insight, and
its formulation required intellectual courage.

By 1799 or 1800 Hegel had extended it to Judaism, described, in a
passage full of invective and irony, as the honoring of a jealous God
who claims sole power and before whom all else is as nought, who
therefore cripples all urges toward genuine accomplishment in real
encounter with the world (Knox, pp. 182–205; Nohl, pp. 243–60). The
same principle is used in criticism of Kant. Taking up Kant's suggestion that there is no difference between a "shaman of the Tungus" or a
"Vogul with a bear's paw on his head" and a "Connecticut Puritan or
Independent" when they let their worship consist of mere belief in
dogmas or celebration of arbitrary observances (*Rel*, p. 164; *AA*, VI,
176), Hegel adds that there is not much difference between *any* of
them and Kant, with his respect for the demands made by his own
moral reason:

> the difference is not that the former make themselves slaves while the
> latter is free, but that the former have their lord outside themselves,
> while the latter carries his lord in himself, yet at the same time is his
> own slave. (Knox, p. 211; Nohl, p. 266)

Hegel preferred to attach himself to the other pole of Kant's ethics, disposition, which cannot really be commanded because it must come forth spontaneously, gladly, from within. But he rejected entirely Kant's view that this disposition, once it comes into being, corresponds to the moral law. The moral law is *universal* in form, it is always and essentially a *concept*, while the disposition of love is something *particular*, and although it can be stated under the logical form of a command this is really alien to it; love has such power that it fulfills the law by making it lose its form as law altogether (Knox, pp. 212–15; Nohl, pp. 266–68).

This appears to be an admirable statement of the Christian principle of love as against Jewish and Kantian legalism. But we should not overlook what Hegel (or anyone else who stresses love in opposition to law) loses in the process: the possibility of acknowledging a *continuing tension* between demand and fulfillment, expressed on one side in a sense of guilt and on the other in eschatological striving, both of which keep Kant's thought relevant to theology. Hegel tends, in these early writings, to dismiss guilt:

> Piety and sin are two concepts which in our sense of the words the Greeks lacked; for us the former is a disposition which acts from respect for God as lawgiver, and the latter is an action in contravention of a divine command. (Knox, p. 164; Nohl, pp. 228–29)

Where Kant saw the need of some kind of justification or satisfaction to make up for the shortcomings that remained despite the goodness of one's disposition, Hegel's solution was to abolish the problem altogether by invoking the term *reconciliation* (*Versöhnung*). The contrast between these two views of salvation is made explicit in a powerful section of "The Spirit of Christianity and Its Fate," anticipating much of Nietzsche and Freud, not to mention Tillich on the theological side, for it examines the psychodynamics of alienation and reconciliation. Whereas the justice of universal, transcendent law is inexorable in its demands, fate or destiny (*Schicksal*) is the rebound of the trespasser's own deed upon himself, taking place entirely within the realm of vital relationships. "And life can heal its wounds again; the severed, hostile life can return into itself again and annul the bungling achievement of a trespass, can annul the law and punishment" (Knox, p. 230; Nohl, p. 281).

Thus the subjectivity of the disposition of love, and the vitality of human relationships, carry within them the power of reconciliation and accomplish what the moral law and its legal justice are unable to do. Yet reconciliation does not come easily, for it is dependent upon a proper balance in all the conditions of life, all the dynamics of the heart. Even Jesus and the early Christian movement, contrary to all that is claimed for them, were unable to achieve full reconciliation, for they also were subject to the common fate of their age:

> The Kingdom of God is not of this world, only it makes a great differ-
> ence for that Kingdom whether this world is actually present in opposi-
> tion to it, or whether its opposition does not exist but is only a possibil-
> ity. The former was in fact the case, and it was with full knowledge of
> this that Jesus suffered at the hands of the state. Hence with this
> [passive] relation to the state one great element in a living union is cut
> away; for the members of the Kingdom of God one important bond of
> association is snapped . . . It is true that from the idea of the Kingdom
> of God all the relationships established in a political order are excluded;
> these rank infinitely lower than the living bonds within the divine
> group, and by such a group they can only be despised. But since the
> state was there and neither Jesus nor his following could annul it, the
> fate of Jesus and his following (which remained true to him in this
> matter) remains a loss of freedom, a restriction of life, passivity under
> the domination of an alien might which was despised but which ceded
> to Jesus without conditions the little that he wanted from it—existence
> among his people. (Knox, p. 284; Nohl, pp. 327–28)

But even the life of his own people was entangled in the net of a legalism that he had to shun.

> The result was that he could find freedom only in the void. Every modi-
> fication of life was in bonds, and therefore Jesus isolated himself from
> his mother, his brothers, and his kinfolk. He might love no wife, beget
> no children; he might not become either a father of a family or a fel-
> low-citizen to enjoy a common life with his fellows. The fate of Jesus
> was that he had to suffer from the fate of his people; either he had to
> make that fate his own, to bear its necessity and share its joy, to unite
> his spirit with his people's but to sacrifice his own beauty, his connec-
> tion with the divine, or else he had to repel his nation's fate from him-
> self but submit to a life undeveloped and without pleasure in itself.
> (Knox, p. 285; Nohl, p. 328)

So Jesus, in the course of his encounter with his people and their leaders, had to lay bare their spirit of hostility to him, without expectation of their conversion, and concentrated his energies on the formation of a small circle of disciples.

The fate of his followers was a slightly different one. They withdrew even from the vital confrontation Jesus had had with his surroundings and became an isolated sectarian community, dreading contact with the wider world. Since their "love" was unable to develop into a full and organic "life" which would bind them together in comprehensive relationships, they had to find the source of their unity in the picture of the resurrected Jesus on which they continued to be dependent, as supplying what was lacking in "a love that was unliving" (Knox, pp. 294–95; Nohl, pp. 336–37). Therefore they continued to experience an "endless, unquenchable, and unappeased longing," unsatisfiable because its object was still only an individual, and religion was still prevented from becoming a complete and self-sustaining "life" (Knox, pp. 300–1; Nohl, p. 341). Hegel's distaste for Christianity in these years is reminiscent of men in late antiquity like Celsus, Porphyry, and Julian, who were unable to forsake classical culture with its political loyalties, its rich ethos, and its varied religious cults, and who despised Christianity and attacked it with hostility because it dared to question these things and separated itself from them.

In these early discussions there are many anticipations of things to come. In the *Phenomenology* and then in the *Philosophy of Religion* he gives a similar picture of Jewish religion as an impotent intensification of the contrast between God and man, without resolution; of the disintegration of Greek culture and the shattering of its imperfect deities as leading people to a sense of total loss; of the Christian movement, and especially Catholicism, as a mistaken attempt to avoid the inward reality of the Spirit and hold on instead to Jesus in his sensuous immediacy, first through belief in the resurrection, then also through pilgrimages, relics, and the Crusaders' fight for the Holy Sepulchre. These insights have continued to have an immense influence upon historians and upon Christian demythologizers as well as the debunkers of religion altogether. Hegel never abandoned, furthermore, his distrust of the more heroic but separatist aspects of Christianity and his hope that its best insights could be expressed more adequately in the highest form of civil society, the State, where the inward and the outward, freedom and participation in the concrete will of a whole people, would be fully reconciled.

Does this stand, then, as the last word about Hegel's view of religion, stated only somewhat more circumspectly in his published writings? There have always been those who think so. In our own time Walter Kaufmann has put forward a vigorous and sustained argument that Hegel's real view was that, when the tensions and crippling antitheses within life are resolved, it will be seen that everything lapses back into the human spirit.[27] What Hegel says in the so-called early theological writings suggests that they are, as Kaufmann says, "anti-theological" instead, for in them Hegel, the disillusioned theology student, is testing Christianity and the Christian conception of God and finds them wanting. If these early writings can be taken as a clue to the meaning of the later Hegel, then Kaufmann has made his case; they are of comfort only to those Christians who take a sentimental view of love, for they really anticipate the kind of merging of the finite and the infinite, the sacred and the profane, that becomes explicit in Feuerbach and in the "death of God" theology of Thomas Altizer.

But when all that has been said, it still seems to me that Hegel grew beyond the largely negative position stated in those early writings. Indeed, most of his *philosophical* development came during the years just *after* the termination of this phase of anti-theological writing, when Hegel began wrestling with the constant stream of writings coming from Fichte and Schelling which raised the philosophical problem of subject and object and their ultimate grounding. At some point, probably in 1802 with the writing of "Glauben und Wissen," he turned away from the subjectivism of the romantics and attempted to plot a better course[28]—not, however, by rejecting the earlier perspective, but by following it through to the end. He acknowledges that the way of subjectivity leads to an infinite striving and a loss of the comfortable distinction between a world of objects and an identifiable self, a "speculative Good Friday," but then finds the original concern for wholeness

27. Kaufmann, *Hegel*, pp. 58–63, 119, 162; cf. also the earlier essay, "The Young Hegel and Religion."
28. Rohrmoser, *Subjektivität und Verdinglichung*, pp. 75 ff.; "Theologische Bedeutung," pp. 105 ff. Cf. Emanuel Hirsch, "Die Beisetzung der Romantiker in Hegels Phänomenologie," *Die idealistische Philosophie und das Christentum* (Göttingen: Vandenhoeck und Ruprecht, 1926), pp. 117–39.

and for knowledge by participation being resurrected, with a new rationality and freedom, in absolute truth.

To be sure, even the published writings upon which Hegel's reputation was built during his own time are theologically ambiguous, so that it was and remains possible to interpret them in a variety of ways, from the atheistic to the pantheistic and even the theistic. The interpretations that take their bearings from the *Phenomenology* stress the priority of human history and tend toward an identification of Spirit with the successive shapes assumed by human subjectivity, leading toward the eventual distillation of pure Spirit in knowledge. Those that operate from the later works must be somewhat more open to speculation, philosophy's looking back over the process to discover its perfect rationality. But what, exactly, is discovered? That God and man have always been essentially identical? Or that man has somehow *become* God during the history of spirit? Or that union with God is a possibility still subject to human decision and action?

In the last analysis we must simply acknowledge, I think, that Hegel was working as a philosopher, which for him meant devising a method and conceptual framework for the rational knowledge of *whatever* is real. Such a method and conceptual framework could be compatible with a wide range of assertions about God, man, society, and the world, and it would be a mistake to suppose that he foreclosed any possibility in advance. We must think of Hegel in company with those other epoch-making philosophers—Aristotle, Descartes, and Whitehead are chief among them—whose greatest influence has been to teach a new way to think, and who as a consequence stimulated widely diverse assertions about the shape of reality among their followers. A method rather than a set of dogmas was the focus of Hegel's concern, and not only is it difficult, it may even be irrelevant to search out his own actual assumptions.

Perhaps the chief reason for the widespread hesitancy to regard Hegel as a theologian is the fact that he retained his early critical attitude toward religion, viewing it as too authoritarian (because it relies upon what is given from without) and too subjective (because it always remains in the medium of feeling and imagination)—in a word, as mythic. Religion, he seems to have thought, is surmounted in the practical realm by politics, which tests out the veiled intuitions of religion in the real world, and in the speculative realm by philosophy, which brings them to full conceptual clarity. Yet we ought to respect the originality of Feuerbach, who, as Marx said, stood Hegel on his head, or rather on his feet since he had been upside down; his convictions should not be read back into Hegel. In the last analysis it seems more credible to suppose that Hegel's policy was not to reduce God to man but rather, as he himself often suggests, to bring man up to participation in the inner life of God, the infinite Subject whose perfection consists in his self-relatedness as Spirit.

It is undeniable that during his professional career Hegel took an interest in theological problems, demonstrated not only in his lectures on the philosophy of religion and on the proofs for God's existence but in several published writings.[29] His contemporaries—with the notable exception of Heine, who was uncannily sensitive to hidden possibilities for inverted meaning—took him at his word and saw him, not exactly as a Christian theologian, for that was not his *métier*, but as a philosopher who had indicated some interesting links between traditional Christian themes and the results of philosophical speculation, indeed, had made the latter grow out of the former.[30]

This can be shown, I think, from those very passages which furnished Feuerbach and Marx the materials for their critique of the religious impulse. In both the *Phenomenology* and the *Philosophy of Religion* it is obvious that the stage of folk culture and folk religion, what

29. See his preface to Hinrichs' *Religionsphilosophie* (1822) and his long and sympathetic review of Göschel's *Aphorismen* (1829), both reprinted in *Berliner Schriften, 1818–1831*, volume XI of the *Sämmtliche Werke, Neue kritische Ausgabe* (Hamburg: Felix Meiner, 1956).

30. For the theological overtones of Hegel's thought see Georg Lasson, *Einführung in Hegels Religionsphilosophie* (Leipzig: Teubner, 1930); Karl Barth's chapter on Hegel in *Die protestantische Theologie im 19. Jahrhundert* (Zollikon/Zurich: Evangelischer Verlag, 1946), translated under the title *Protestant Thought: From Rousseau to Ritschl* (London: SCM Press, 1959); Jörg Splett, *Die Trinitätslehre G. W. F. Hegels* (Symposion, XX; Freiburg and Munich: Karl Alber, 1965); Stephen G. Crites, "The Gospel according to Hegel," *Journal of Religion*, XLVI (1966); 246–63; William C. Shepherd, "Hegel as a Theologian," *Harvard Theological Review*, XLI (1968): 583–602; Emil Fackenheim, *The Religious Dimension in Hegel's Thought* (Bloomington, Ind.: Indiana University Press, 1967); Wolf-Dieter Marsch, *Gegenwart Christi in der Gesellschaft. Eine Studie zu Hegels Dialektik* (Forschungen zur Geschichte und Lehre des Protestantismus; Munich: Chr. Kaiser, 1965); and Hans Küng, *Menschwerdung Gottes. Eine Einführung in Hegels theologische Denken als Prolegomena zu einer künftigen Christologie* (Ökumenische Forschungen, II, 1; Freiburg: Herder, 1970). A comprehensive summary of the issues raised in the recent literature is to be found in Wolf-Dieter Marsch, "Logik des Kreuzes. Über Sinn und Grenzen einer theologischen Berufung auf Hegel," *Evangelische Theologie*, XXVIII (1968); 57–82.

he calls *Sittlichkeit* (ethos) or "objective spirit," is by no means the highest, for despite its attractiveness it is an imperfect development of spirit. The ego finds itself only in the ethos of the community, the latter is the only "substance," the only focus of consciousness; all individuality, all concrete personal activity, is made a function of the self-sufficient "essence" of the community, which rules all (*Phen*, pp. 317–42, 457–87). But when trust in this substance is shattered, individuality comes forth with full intensity. That is the situation that arose with the breakdown of the older Greek ethos, expressed most adequately in Roman law, where concrete national heritage disappears and is supplanted by the "abstract person" of law (*Phen*, pp. 501 ff., 537 ff., 751 ff.). The difficulty is that this abstract, uprooted individuality leaves man empty and unrealized; the feeling of despair at losing one's world, the resorption of everything into consciousness, the return of spirit to itself and the agonizing awareness of its own lack of sufficiency, leave it yearning for something better (*Phen*, pp. 748–55).

If we have any doubt that Hegel takes this to be a development leading man on toward God rather than his own subjectivity, we can look at another passage in the *Phenomenology* which presents a higher stage in the realization of the human spirit: his description of the pietists' and the romantics' goal of "beauty of soul," spirit resting within its own immediacy, untroubled about any supposed opposition between duty and inclination (*Phen*, pp. 652–54). Hegel is obviously thinking of romantics like Jacobi, Novalis, and Schleiermacher, but the description also fits the position he himself had held a few years before, down to the expression "beauty of soul" (cf. Knox, pp. 234–41; Nohl, pp. 285–91); thus in criticizing them he is also secretly reprimanding the Hegel of the unpublished writings. Here something much like the "unhappy self-consciousness" is brought to explicit formulation by the victims themselves, as subjectivity lost within itself, having no object except what is an echo of its own voice, returning to itself only to find each moment of consciousness dissolving into another; however confidently and defiantly it asserts itself, it is constantly divided and diminished, sensing its individuality as longing (*Phen*, p. 666). By this time Hegel has gone well beyond his earlier glorification of "life" and "love" and has discovered the bankruptcy of that dependence on immediacy, for it will never yield more than the finitude of the individual subject. He comes to stress, therefore, not immediacy but the "mediacy" or objectivity that is effected through conceptualization; the goal of the pilgrimage of finite spirit is to know Absolute Spirit, to know even oneself *in* Absolute Spirit, and to know that this knowledge is Absolute Spirit's knowing itself through the human spirit. Hegel did not lose his concern for subjectivity. Even though he criticized Schleiermacher unmercifully for limiting religion to immediate feeling he was ready to acknowledge the place of feeling and conviction in religion, so long as they were shaped by objective factors. But he had done with pure subjectivity and vitality.

Just as clearly he had moved beyond the expectation of finding an anchor for subjectivity in *ethos*, the participation of the individual in the life of a community. With the downfall of the older Greek culture the dwelling place of the human spirit, Hegel believed, had shifted from "substance" (the objective, communal ethos) to "subjectivity," and from then on it would be inauthentic to have ethos on any other terms than those imposed by self-consciousness as it *produces its own* objects or *gives itself freely* to them (*Phen*, pp. 711, 750). Of course he affirmed the public task of free men in the State, which climaxes his *Philosophy of Right*. In this sense Feuerbach and Marx, with their confidence that self-alienation would be overcome through wholehearted and fearless participation in the practical tasks of society, are legitimate successors to Hegel. But the State presupposes the development of a fully conscious and explicitly willed freedom: spirit must first have overcome its self-alienation, which for Hegel means achieving a perfect coincidence of vital subjectivity and conceptual objectivity, and only then it can safely resume contact with the social process.

All of this is by way of argument that the pilgrimage of the spirit as Hegel presents it in the *Phenomenology* and the *Philosophy of Religion* leads not toward God's reduction to man but toward man's participation in God. This can be seen in the way he presents those moments of greatest tension which are the birthpangs of a higher insight, for from their lines of stress it is clear that a resolution "from above" is alone satisfactory. This is the case with both those chapters of human history which are taken to be most indicative: the "religion of individuality" which comes out of the tradition of Israel, with its modern counterpart, Kantian morality; and the "unhappy self-consciousness" that followed the breakdown of ancient culture, together with its modern counterpart, "beauty of soul."

Hegel's presentation of Israelite religion, the "religion of individuality," has some surprising anticipations of Kierkegaard (and since S.K. will always haunt the travels of Hegel's shade, we must be aware of him). This religion catches man on the way between his original potentialities, lost in the dimness of natural immediacy, and their full and proper realization through the mediation of consciousness and freedom. It is a sign of man's dignity that he cannot be "naturally" good, for it is of the "nature" of spirit that it goes beyond its own immediacy, ceases to be merely natural. But when he wills, the content of his willing is not the fulfillment of his task as spirit but is merely the satisfying of his natural inclinations; thus his particularity comes into contradiction with his true essence.[31] But it is only through this contrast between what he is and what he ought to be that man gains self-knowledge, the "knowledge of good and evil" of which Genesis 3 speaks, for good and evil are known together, through the bifurcation and contradiction in man's own life. He becomes aware of himself and of his own freedom as an infinite task, and therefore with an infinite subjectivity that is absent in the religions of nature; the bifurcation and opposition within a single subject is experienced as an infinite pain, individualizing and interiorizing and deepening him (Lasson, III, 109–21). The same discovery, Hegel thinks, was made during the breakdown of Greek religion, when for somewhat different reasons the subject returned to itself and discovered its infinite contradiction.

The contradiction is not the last word, to be sure; it is built out of an opposition between man's actuality and his own potentiality, and it is to be expected that the potentiality will function as a precondition for reconcilation, that the contradiction at its most intense will be a direct preparation for reconciliation. But this does not mean that the contra-

31. Following Kant, at least in part, he distinguishes between (a) the "natural" will, immediate impulse, (b) *Wille*, the capacity to respond to reason, (c) *Willkür*, the abstract, purely formal indeterminacy of the will, manifested in the arbitrary choice of this or that specific content, and (d) "actual willing," which, since it is always a concrete act, cannot be purely evil, as Milton's Satan shows (Lasson, III, 105–9, 117 n.). Similarly in the *Philosophy of Right* he says that *Willkür* is constituted by an abstract, purely formal reflection of the Ego into itself, and its encounter with specific contents that come from outside the will, from sensation, emotion, or thought (§ 15). He sees original sin as the refusal of this arbitrary freedom to live according to rational principles—a state of affairs which ought not to be, yet which has a certain inevitability because of the conjunction between man's undeveloped, merely natural character and the universal scope of his rationality, for when man *wills* the natural, it is no longer the goodness of nature, but evil and irrationality (§ 139).

diction is mere appearance, or a mistaken estimate by man of himself. It discloses something of permanent importance about man, central to Hegel's entire philosophy of spirit. Even to say that this awareness is "abstract"—always a term of reproach with Hegel—is not to suggest that it ought to be collapsed into the concrete actuality that already is. "Abstractness" is the characteristic of thinking (and willing) which reaches beyond finite particularity but has not yet arrived at a higher object and thus is left in a condition of longing and striving, still without content. To use Hegel's own terminology, abstract thinking can bring forth a "conception" (*Begriff*) of what man is implicitly and should be in full actuality, but this conception is not yet an "idea" (*Idee*), for an idea has real content and productive power. Spirit is always (even in God) a movement from thinking to conception to realization in idea; perhaps the best illustration is the familiar process of reflecting on options, projecting conceptions of the way we would like something to be, and then resolving upon some course and aligning our own being in accordance with it (cf. Lasson, III, 10–12, 38, 56–57; *Philosophy of Right*, §§ 7–13, 21–28). In God, who is pure thinking, *actus purus*, light without shadow, this takes place without breaking the unity of his life. In man, however, the conception is seen as an infinite task, without possessing the immediate resources for giving it reality through one's own thinking and willing.

This far Hegel can follow Kant. What makes him discontent with him, and always sets them apart, is that for Kant the demands of moral reason stand in perpetual contrast with man's willing, so that they meet only at the end of an infinite progress; man will always be in need of vicarious "satisfaction," and therefore

> the non-moral consciousness is to pass for moral, its contingent knowledge and will to be accepted as fully sufficing, and happiness to be its lot as a matter of grace. (*Phen*, p. 644)

—a fair, if not exact, description of Kant's views in Book II of the *Religion*. This, Hegel thinks, is "dissembling."

The step beyond Kant comes in trying to spell out the possibility of a *real reconciliation with God*. Kant, of course, was quite unsure of the grace of the Holy Spirit and denied that there can be any immediate experience even of the human self, let alone God and his presence. Hegel was willing to venture more, and to say that the ideal archetype of a true humanity involves a *unity between God and man.* The impetus probably came from Fichte, whose thought Hegel found the most congenial during his formative years in the first decade of the century. In one famous passage Fichte says that the "element" in which true life is sustained is Thought, the divine life itself, God acting through man, and that the goal of Christianity properly understood is just such a unity of divine and human being.[32] Whatever Fichte meant by it (and that was itself a matter of controversy), Hegel did not mean an identity of God and man in every respect, a self-deification of the human spirit. They are distinct, although they are also mutually immanent, since there is a real relation from both sides, God knowing himself through man and man knowing even himself in God.

As Hegel discusses it in the passage on "the actuality of reconciliation" (Lasson, III, 130–42), reconciliation is something that the individual must achieve for himself, and yet he cannot accomplish it out of the resources of his own individuality, bound as he is by evil and unable to overcome it in his finitude. He must be raised out of his natural will and make a union with God the principal goal of his willing, and yet he cannot begin from himself. Therefore this human self-actualization (*Setzung*) presupposes (*voraussetzt*) a prior actuality of reconciliation. This is accomplished first of all in the eternal activity of God, as he distinguishes himself from himself in the Word and reaffirms himself in Love. But this eternal activity of God, and the accomplishment of reconciliation within himself, already encompasses man in all his finitude, his otherness from God, even his alienation from God:

> the unity of divine and human nature has significance for the determination not only of human nature but also of the divine, for all difference, all finitude, is a moment, however transitory it may be, in the process of divine nature, and this develops though it remains grounded in itself. (Lasson, III, 131)

Clearly Hegel thinks of the reconciliation of the divine and the human as one that takes place within God—that is why he calls it a divine *idea*, implying that it is already fulfilled, in ideal reality, within God. In effect Hegel makes of the idea what Kant said Plato made of it

---

32. Johann Gottlieb Fichte, *Die Anweisung zum seligen Leben, oder auch die Religionslehre* (1806), sixth lecture (*Sämmtliche Werke*, V [Berlin: Veit, 1845], 483–84).

(*Critique of Pure Reason*, A 313), the archetype of the changing appearances of things, which Kant, however, could not affirm for his own part. What makes it different from Kant's "ideal archetype of humanity" is that it is *not* merely an intention and a demand projected into the infinite future from before the creation of the world; it takes into account the actual world as it goes its way outside God, even man in his opposition to God, and resolves every problem first of all within God himself. It is perhaps rather like what a more straightforwardly religious type of language calls God's mercy and faithfulness toward man. A good biblical counterpart to Hegel's doctrine of "idea" is to be found in Heb. 6:13, where it is said that God, in making a promise, "swore upon himself" since there was no one greater for him to swear it upon: in other words, the purpose is first conceived and then is given a guaranteed content by God's own commitment to it.

But of course the "idea" must be communicated to persons and take effect within their own lives. If this is to happen, Hegel thinks, the unity of divine and human natures, already resolved within God, must first be "represented" (*vorgestellt*) in an individual *other* than the ones who come to discover it, and this, of course, is the significance of Jesus. What makes such representation necessary is that they, occupied with their accustomed sphere of worldly activity, are unaware of their intrinsic potentialities; what makes it possible is that the sensible world is not alien to spirit but is one facet of its own life, and even the finitude and weakness of Jesus' humanity is not inconsistent with the intrinsic unity of God and man. When Jesus exhibits, in his finite particularity, a fully achieved unity between God and man, he acts out the message that God is not alien to man and that man is even being taken up into God's life. It is appropriate, Hegel thinks, that there be *one* individual who represents the idea, for the idea also is one, concrete, and real in God, not an abstraction from a multiplicity of individuals. And he does not do this merely as a kind of externalized symbol. Hegel describes Jesus as a "prophet," one who speaks in God's behalf, directly to others, so that in him they come into immediate encounter with God (Lasson, III, 153), and the directness and immediacy of this encounter is the basis of what he calls "certitude" or "conviction" (*Gewissheit*), the manifestation of truth *for the subject* and in relation to its own destiny (Lasson, III, 141–42, 154–55). Thereby the human subject becomes able, for the first time, to reconcile itself with God and enter the "kingdom of the Spirit" through personal participation, which is, of course, the center of gravity in Hegel's thinking.

The picture that Hegel presents of the "kingdom of the Spirit" is not excessively triumphalist. In his discussion of baptism, for example, he remarks that the child is born into a situation in which God is reconciled and evil is overcome, but nevertheless spirit must still be reborn in the face of continuing sin:

> This rebirth is no longer that infinite sadness which was the birthpang of the spiritual community, but there is still opposition from man's particularity, his special interests, passions, selfishness. The natural heart, in which man is imprisoned, is the enemy which is still to be fought. The real and infinite sorrow of his inadequacy in relation to God, though it is not spared him, is softened; but this is no longer the real struggle out of which the spiritual community originally grew. (*Werke* [1832], XII, 270; cf. Lasson, III, 205)

The point is that now the natural will, with its isolated self-seeking, can be surrendered in man's inward life. There will still be deeds and impulses which are incommensurate with this inward actuality, but God looks on the heart, "the substantial will, the inmost, all-comprehending subjectivity of man, his inward, true, earnest willing" (Lasson, III, 203). What continues to set Hegel apart from Kant, who also acknowledged just such a fundamental change of heart despite the persistence of weakness and passion, is that Kant had to rely solely upon an imputed justification to bring the tarnished reality of man into harmony with the majesty of the ideal, while Hegel, always concerned to bridge that gap but unable in all honesty to carry through his youthful attempts to do it from man's side, saw reconciliation being achieved within the divine life, in God's own interaction with the world process and human history, and made man a knowing and willing participant within it.

Perhaps Hegel's chief contribution was to give new impetus to this striving after a higher and more internalized form of Christianity. He was not the first to do it—his conception of the "kingdom of the Spirit" is obviously influenced by Lessing, who revived the hope of Joachim of Flora for a "third age" and made it respectable for the first time—nor was he the last, for people like Norman O. Brown and Thomas Altizer have still been advancing similar visions in our own day, though more in the style of Feuerbach or the younger Hegel. Without doubt we need to be circumspect in using a theme like this, for it can take many forms, some of them sentimental or fanatical.

Indeed, there is a recurring suspicion that Hegel himself, because he claimed definitive knowledge of the development of spirit, tried prematurely to bring all things to their fulfillment. His left-wing followers and critics could not rest so easily with the existing society and its religion, preferring to see in them alienation rather than reconciliation (although even they were tempted to see reconciliation just around the corner, after the next revolution in life or consciousness). But it would be false to Hegel if we were to attempt to transform his perspective on the present and future into a perpetual dialectic of cross and resurrection (Marsch), for this would be to make it into a theology of the "second article"; or a utopian ideal which holds out the vision of something new to come (Bloch, Moltmann), for this would be to make it into a theology of the "first article."[33] His own special emphasis ought to be respected, and the *political* critique of Hegel should not be permitted to obscure the *religious* point he was making. He felt that the decisive insights had already been arrived at ("God has no more secrets" [Lasson, I, 75]), the ultimate reconciliation begun ("an eternal kingdom of God has been established," "the holy Spirit as such lives eternally in the Church" [Lasson, III, 231]), although he also recognized that the flow of history goes on, the need for human action remains, and religion continues to outrun the actual world and indicate better possibilities for the future.[34]

The leading insight is unexceptionable: it is, quite simply, that reconciliation and renewal, even fulfillment, can and must occur in human life, and that they are more likely to occur in the medium of subjectivity than in natural or social relationships. The point is an authentic one in Christianity: that the power of the last time is already at work through the Spirit, effecting a real transformation in the human condition. It is one well worth giving special emphasis, particularly in the

33. Such intra-mural debates within the broadly Hegelian tradition, up into our own day, are the theme of a helpful book by Peter Cornehl, *Die Zukunft der Versöhnung. Eschatologie und Emanzipation in der Aufklärung, bei Hegel und in der Hegelschen Schule* (Göttingen: Vandenhoeck und Ruprecht, 1971); see especially the concluding portions.

34. For this aspect of Hegel's thought, see Fackenheim, pp. 211–12; Marsch, pp. 201–3; and Küng, pp. 289–91, 389–90.

Protestant world, where justification by faith is often taken to be the sole norm and there is reluctance to think that anything interesting or important can happen within man himself. One can acknowledge that all accomplishments are partial and fragmentary ones, and yet affirm that the final redemption is already taking place, that it is not totally in the realm of hope or longing. It is not altogether outrageous, either, to suggest that man can and should free himself from external authority and rely increasingly upon insights he himself has come to, decisions he himself has arrived at. Paul ascribed precisely this kind of authority to the person who is guided by the Spirit. To be sure, Hegel tends to look away from the person of Jesus with unseemly haste, as from a mere stage along the way toward the insights and achievements of his own age. Yet, even in this way he offers testimony to the relevance of the Christian message to the modern temper and gives a much-needed reminder to Christians and non-Christians alike that independence of mind, readiness for decision, transformation of heart, even union with God, are set before everyone—and that they do not merely hover above us as an unattainable ideal, or outside us in the enigmatic figure of Jesus, but are addressed to us as a promise, and thus as a task, to be fulfilled in our own life.

4. The Archetype Christology in Theological Debate

The full digesting of the problems raised by the three giants came in the generation following Schleiermacher and Hegel, during the 1830s and 1840s. It would be tedious to tell the whole tale, and it can be found readily enough in two works of that era (or rather in their final sections, since both are massive doctrinal histories), written by Isaac August Dorner and Ferdinand Christian Baur, rival participants in the debate.[35] Dorner was a young *Dozent* at Tübingen in the late 1830s, in direct polemical encounter with Baur. When he asserted—following the principles of the archetype Christology—that the incarnation was a

---

35. I. A. Dorner, *Entwicklungsgeschichte der Lehre von der Person Christi* (first edition Stuttgart, 1839, and many editions thereafter). The second edition of 1845–53 was translated under the title *History of the Development of the Doctrine of the Person of Christ* (Edinburgh: T. & T. Clark, 1878). Only volume II of the Second Division is immediately pertinent to our subject. The opposition statement was soon issued by F. C. Baur in *Die christliche Lehre von der Dreieinigkeit und Menschwerdung Gottes in ihrer geschichtlichen Entwicklung* (Tübingen: C. F. Osiander, 1843). Only the last two hundred-some pages of volume III concern the modern phase. For a more recent survey of the period and its debates, see Emanuel Hirsch's *Geschichte der neuern evangelischen Theologie*, V, 362–414.

suitable climax and completion of human history, it was in answer to the speculations of Baur and his pupil Strauss, which—again on the basis of the archetype Christology—called into question the possibility of incarnation at all.

We have had occasion already to take note of Baur's criticism of Schleiermacher in 1827, based on a conviction, derived from Schelling, that the ideal archetype cannot be adequately expressed in a finite individual. In view of Baur's unchanging assent to that speculative principle, we must suppose that his assertion, first in the comments on Schleiermacher and then in *Die christliche Gnosis*, that modern speculative theology—Schelling, Schleiermacher, Hegel—was "Gnostic" in character (proceeding as it did from reason rather than history) to be not an attack on it but an unobtrusive enlistment of support for the position he personally held, namely, a combination of the speculative and historical methods which would keep the two aspects distinct and unconfused, even divided and separated from each other.

Baur's favorite, most brilliant, and most notorious student during those years was David Friedrich Strauss. Despite the legend that his views are somehow the logical outcome of Hegel's philosophy of religion, all the evidence suggests that Schelling was the first major influence upon him, and that he could have got almost all the elements of the position he publicized so forcefully in his *Leben Jesu* of 1835 a full ten years before, when he was Baur's pupil in the "seminary" at Blaubeuren, just prior to their both coming to Tübingen.[36] Strauss began to read Hegel about 1829, and soon considered himself a Hegelian; Baur read him only about 1834, and at Strauss's instigation.[37] Although it is true that they were deeply influenced by Hegel in many respects, in their Christology the Hegelian language did little more than clothe a perspective based solidly on Schelling.

Strauss wielded a two-edged sword against traditional Christology. From Baur and others he had learned the discipline of historical research, and his *Leben Jesu* is generally considered to be the first real contribution to the quest for the historical Jesus. He analyzed the traditions as an expression, in imagery and legend, of the consciousness of the primitive Christian community, and felt that when these were

36. Müller, pp. 196, 213–15.
37. Hodgson, p. 23.

stripped away he could begin to sift the facts about Jesus that had also come through in the traditions. The depiction that he emerged with, although it conflicted with the usual beliefs, certainly was not unrecognizable. The furor was caused not merely by his historical findings but just as much by the conclusions he drew in a *Schlussabhandlung* or concluding dissertation. He could not see that Jesus was unique in any way, he said, except as giving the "occasion" for the rise of an awareness of the idea of divine humanity, an idea which remained clothed, however, in mythic forms and was projected upon Jesus out of the need to link it with some concrete individual. The philosophical principle upon which he based this conclusion (backed up, of course, by the historical facts as he saw them) was the one taken from Schelling: "The idea is not wont to lavish all its fullness on one exemplar, and be niggardly toward all others." Once speculative reason becomes aware of this truth, the historical imagery which clothed it, together with the historical individual who occasioned its rise, become "only the faint image of a dream which belongs only to the past." It is necessary, then, to restate the truth conveyed by Christianity (and once again we must quote from the classic translation by George Eliot [§ 151]):

This is the key to the whole of Christology, that, as subject of the predicate which the church assigns to Christ, we place, instead of an individual, an idea, but an idea which has an existence in reality, not in the mind only, like that of Kant. In an individual, a God-man, the properties and functions which the church ascribes to Christ contradict themselves; in the idea of the race, they perfectly agree. Humanity is the union of the two natures—God become man, the infinite manifesting itself in the finite, and the finite spirit remembering its infinitude; it is the child of the visible Mother and the invisible Father, Nature and Spirit; it is the worker of miracles, in so far as in the course of human history the spirit more and more completely subjugates nature, both within and around man, until it lies before him as the inert matter on which he exercises his active power; it is the sinless existence, for the course of its development is a blameless one, pollution cleaves to the individual only and does not touch the race or its history. It is Humanity that dies, rises, and ascends to heaven, for from the negation of its phenomenal life there ever proceeds a higher spiritual life; from the suppression of its mortality as a personal, national, and terrestrial spirit, arises its union with the infinite spirit of the heavens. By faith in this Christ, especially in his death and resurrection, man is justified before God; that is, by the kindling within him of the idea of Humanity, the

individual man participates in the divinely human life of the species.
Now the main element of that idea is that the negation of the merely
natural and sensual life, which is itself the negation of the spirit (the
negation of negation, therefore), is the sole way to true spiritual life.

Baur continued to hold the same principles that had influenced his
pupil. He thought that the ideal archetype must remain infinite and
unconditioned, that it can be realized only in the *whole* of humanity,
not in a single individual (*DM*, III, 885). He suggested (*DM*, III,
963–66; 996–99) that the history of the world, which is the same as
the divine life, would stop if ever there were a perfect embodiment of
the absolute idea, since history is constituted by the tension between
what is already and what is not yet, between the actual and the ideal.
In any case, he felt, it is impossible to suppose a finite subjectivity
completely determined by the being of God. The idea is always *more*
than any individual, and in each individual there must be some degree
of difference from the idea, "*das Nichtseyn der Idee*," even if only a
"minimum." (This, I might say, exhibits Baur's difference from Hegel,
or else his failure to understand Hegel's doctrine of spirit, for spirit—in
this case man's—would be able to go out of itself toward that which is
other than itself—in this case God—without being totally absorbed,
since it remains a distinct focus of activity and is even fulfilled in its
openness toward the other. Baur's line of thought here, as elsewhere,
seems to be derived from Schelling, for whom the Absolute needs to be
unfolded in the multiplicity of the finite, and can be related to any particular thing only as the whole to a part.) Baur also suggests that the
idea, by its very character, must apply generally to *all* persons, and if it
were to be perfectly actualized in an individual, then other individuals
would somehow be excluded. (This is a weak argument from every
point of view except Schelling's, and it conflicts with the rather general
assumption that the ideal archetype is applicable to *all* individuals, *as*
thinking and willing individuals and not as organic parts of the human
race.)

In *Die christliche Gnosis*, published in 1835, just before Strauss's
Leben Jesu, Baur said,

> If the God-man as such is the unity of the divine and the human,
> humanity one with God, the historical Christ is humanity in all its mem-
> bers, which together make up the living body of Christ, realizing the

concept of religion, striving onward from earth toward heaven, uniting itself with God. In humanity so conceived, his community which is still growing and receiving the fullness of the Spirit, the God-man Christ is still present in the living truth and actuality of history and celebrates the eternal victory of life over death, the eternal festival of his resurrection and ascension. Thus there is not lacking even to this philosophy of religion [the Hegelian, as presented by Baur] a quite concrete concept of the historical Christ. (*Gnosis*, pp. 720–21)

To that extent Baur agreed openly with Strauss. He had to acknowledge that when one asked the question, "What must be presupposed in the individual person of Christ if, through faith in him as the God-man, the idea of the unity of God and man can be mediated to the consciousness of humanity?" the minimum answer *could* be the one Strauss had given, and it is for historical investigation, not speculation, to say how far he *surpasses* that minimum (*DM*, III, 974).

But Baur thought that the historical evidence warranted something more. A few years earlier, in dealing with the problems raised by the astounding similarities between the Gospels and Philostratus' life of Apollonius of Tyana, he had argued that the latter must be directly derived from the former, because it exhibits no vitality of its own:

> In place of him whom Christianity sets before us as the actually manifested Redeemer of the world, we have here only a sage acting through precept and example; the latter is, furthermore—and this must be the chief perspective—*no living form* but only an image lacking independent reality and the actuality of a human existence, only the faint, shadowy reflection of a living original, without which it seems even the creative thought which called forth that picture would be lacking.[38]

Baur was cautious, however, about the inferences he drew from such arguments. He liked Schleiermacher's suggestion that certitude about Jesus' inward life can be based upon its effects in the Christian consciousness. But from this one could not infer, as Schleiermacher did, that Jesus was in his own person the actualization of the archetype of humanity; that would be to go beyond the evidence. All that one could say is that a new "vital principle" (*Lebensprinzip*) is implanted in human history. Although Jesus can be considered its originator there is

---

38. F. C. Baur, *Apollonius von Tyana und Christus, oder das Verhältnis des Pythagoreismus zum Christenthum* (Tübingen: C. F. Osiander, 1832), p. 162.

no need to suppose that it is personalized in him any more than it is in the Church, for it is only a power that he releases, not identical with himself or limited to himself. "Christ has only the significance of a principle," he wrote, "but is not an absolute [archetypal] personality" (*DM*, III, 880–81).[39]

Most theologians took fright at the line of thought being pursued by Baur and Strauss, and they put forward an alternative, obviously a stopgap designed to forestall such alarming speculations. If the archetypal ideal threatens to float free from the historical individuality of Jesus, then why not give it more ballast so that it is compelled to descend to earth in a particular individual? So during the 1830s, especially after the publication of Strauss's *Life of Jesus* in 1835, a number of "Right Hegelians," churchmen or philosophers who felt that Hegel had indicated the lasting value of the dogmas of the Trinity and the incarnation but that even more could be said along these lines, tried to demonstrate that the idea of divine-human unity *must* be expressed not merely within God, as an entity of reason, but in external earthly fact, in an individual God-man. It goes without saying that for theologians like these the incarnation has a function entirely independent of sin. Thus there was a kind of Scotist revival in the German theology of the 1830s and 1840s, widely influential (extending even to the Catholic theologian Scheeben), and it is probably the immediate source of Karl Barth's Christocentrism. Speculative arguments based on what they thought could be deduced from the eternal idea of a humanity united with God were put forward by Hegelians like Conradi (as early as 1831), Rosenkranz (1836), Schaller, and Göschel (both in 1838). Dorner and his close friend, the Danish theologian Hans Martensen, added a motif drawn from Schelling and Schleiermacher: if the human

39. Cf. the whole passage, pp. 877–86, and the mention (p. 965, n. 20) of the important historical point that the term *principle* was first used by Dorner in characterizing—in order to reproach—Baur's position. The same line of thought was carried on, within the framework of an entire systematic theology, by Alois Emanuel Biedermann of Zurich. He stressed even more than Baur that the new principle or power at work is specifically religious, a relation between finite and infinite Spirit which springs not from an eternal truth of speculation, not even from an anthropological truth about the intrinsic relation of humanity to God, but from a contingent enactment in the self-consciousness of Jesus, actualizing what had been merely potential in human nature and then conveying this new principle of life to all those who belong to his community (see the selections from the second edition of his *Christliche Dogmatik* [Zürich, 1884], in *God and Incarnation in Mid-Nineteenth Century German Theology: G. Thomasius, I. A. Dorner, A. E. Biedermann*, ed. and trans. Claude Welch [New York: Oxford University Press, 1965]).

race is an organically developing whole, whose diversified talents can be exhibited only in the entire development, the "idea" of humanity would be diffused and lost from sight if there were not a "central individual" who could represent in his own inward life "humanity as such," thus giving to the human essence an "intensive" fulfillment (of course its "extensive" fulfillment must still be achieved in the broader life of humanity, or specifically in that portion of it that has been influenced and unified by the God-man).

I do not mean to slight the achievements of these men in theological speculation. But their position must be evaluated in the light of the problems that had been posed. Hegel, it is true, had also asserted that the divine idea ought to be represented in *one* earthly individual, since the idea is complete in and for itself, proceeding from divine thought and not being abstracted from a number of individuals. But it is obvious that Hegel's argument was a purely functional one: *if* the idea is to be *manifested*, then it must be manifested in this way. He did not think that manifestation in a single individual was required *by the idea* for its own completeness, for he suggested that reconciliation is already complete, in one sense, within God himself. The manifestation of the idea is entirely for man's sake, because of his bondage to the natural and his inability to rise out of it. It never becomes an end in itself, for its function is to lead man back toward the idea in its simplicity, and to do this precisely through the tensions set up within the finite by the appearance of this individual:

> Individuality, as something exclusive, is given immediately to the experience of the other, and is the return from the other back to itself. The individuality of the divine idea, the divine idea as *one* man, is fulfilled in actuality only when it begins to have as its counterpart a multiplicity of individuals and leads them back to unity of spirit, to community, and is in it as its common actual self-consciousness. (Lasson, III, 164)

Precisely as individual and exclusive he incorporates others into what he represents, through their rebound from his individuality and their seeking of the universal represented by him. He may even retain his individual function and be the object of a continuing dependence on the part of others (although this is more than Hegel himself was willing to say). Still his exclusiveness is not even for a moment a focusing of the idea upon himself, since the idea applies to all—

From the chalice of this realm of spirits
Foams forth to God his own infinity. (*Phen*, 808; cf. Lasson, III, 132)[40]

Hegel cannot be invoked to support the Christocentrist speculations of some of his admirers, for he took the incarnation chiefly as a symbol of the nature and destiny of all men. The real contribution of the Hegelians and the Hegelianizers among the theologians—a contribution widely, if not quite universally acknowledged—was to place at the center of Christianity the positive relationship between God and man which some of them called the "essential unity of the divine and the human" and which others, cautious of the pantheistic reading that could be given to that expression, preferred to call a "union of God and man."[41]

In the period we are discussing a number of theologians did manage to keep an even keel, and they turn out, to his credit, to be the closest followers of Schleiermacher, men whose program was to "mediate" between Christianity and philosophy, between supernaturalism and rationalism. They saw that the ideal *must* be realized in *every* individual if the purpose of creation is to be fulfilled, and that it is only because humanity in freedom comes to contradict the ideal—thus posing a problem that is insoluble from man's side—that there needs to be a decisive point of reversal in an individual who overcomes sin and thereby represents the ideal in his own person, in communion with

---

40. Hegel liked to quote, with a few modifications, these closing lines of Schiller's "Friendship." His intent, at least at the end of the *Phenomenology*, has often been taken to be atheistic (see especially Alexandre Kojève, *Introduction to the Reading of Hegel: Lectures on the Phenomenology of Spirit*, trans. James H. Nichols, Jr. [New York: Basic Books, 1969], pp. 166–67, and also Kaufmann, *Hegel*, p. 162). But it seems clear that his meaning, which comes out most clearly in the *Lectures on the Philosophy of Religion*, is rather that the person who has grasped God's presence with the certitude of spiritual participation will know that God is immediately present in all men, and that the infinite life of the human spirit is in fact a striving to return to unity with God.

41. Among the Hegelians we could name Marheineke, Baur, Strauss, and Biedermann; among the Hegelianizers, those who utilized Hegel's language to express in more forthright terms an old Christian theme, we could name Dorner and Martensen, and also Carl Ullmann, who acknowledged that modern speculative theology had aided in the formulation of the real "essence of Christianity" (see his "Ueber dem unterscheidenden Charakter des Christenthums, mit Beziehung auf neuere Auffassungsweisen," *Theologische Studien und Kritiken*, XVIII (1845): 7–61, trans. John W. Nevin as a preliminary essay in his *The Mystical Presence* [Philadelphia: J. B. Lippincott & Co., 1846]). Karl Barth's stress on "God for man" and "man for God" is a continuation of the same tradition, more explicitly rooted, of course, in the biblical theme of covenant and basing the union not upon *nature* but upon *decision* and *enactment*.

whom the rest can then move toward the universal goal.[42] It seems
clear enough that this is the only proper outcome of the debate on its
own terms, and it is a position with which all three major figures we
have examined could agree, insofar as they ventured any assertions at
all in Christian theology. It also serves to connect what I have called
the "archetype Christology" with earlier discussions of the pattern of
Christian theology, for the classic question has always concerned the
place of Jesus within the whole of human history, and the archetype
Christology has contributed an illuminating new interest in Jesus'
humanity and its relation to the task set before all.

5. Beyond the Nineteenth Century

What insights have emerged, then, from this new line of inquiry that
I have called the "archetype Christology"? I have been discussing the
key participants in terms of three different emphases: some of them
stress the first article, the general relevance of the archetypal ideal to
all of humanity, often with such intensity that they are unable to indicate how it can be focused, in any unique way, in a particular individual (Kant, Schelling, Baur); some stress the second article, the person
of Jesus and the direct dependence of believers upon him through the
Church (Schleiermacher and the mediating theologians); and some
stress the third article, the real participation of others as well in the
divine life through the Spirit that animates the community (the Hegelians). Although these three perspectives involved their champions in
many debates, we need to exclude none of them, only to deprive each
of its claim to sole truth.

From the Hegelian school at least a few theologians, after being bullied unnecessarily by the limited view of man's capacities that has been

---

42. Baur (*DM*, III, 994–96) names (in order to criticize) Schweizer, Kern, Ullmann, and Weisse; but there are many others who could be added to the list. For
a discussion of the "mediating theologians" in the context of their age—although
only a beginning has been made toward the examination of their individual contributions—see Ragnar Holte, *Die Vermittlungstheologie. Ihre theologischen Grundbe-
griffe kritisch untersucht* (Uppsala: Almquist & Wiksell, 1965): Emanuel Hirsch,
Geschichte der neuern evangelischen Theologie, V, 375–414; and Claude Welch,
Protestant Thought in the Nineteenth Century, vol. I, 1799–1870 (New Haven:
Yale University Press, 1972), chap. 12. Perhaps the best source, written by a man
who was a fellow student with many of them and shared their viewpoint, is Philip
Schaff, *Germany, Its Universities, Theology, and Religion, with Sketches of . . .
Distinguished German Divines of the Age* (Philadelphia: Lindsay and Blakiston;
New York: Sheldon, Blakeman & Co., 1857).

widespread in modern times, have learned to find their way back to the confident style of thought of the era of the fathers. They become capable of thinking of a direct relationship of man to God and to see in the person of Christ a communion with God which is not an absolute exception to the rule but can be approximated to by others, just as the fathers, as we saw earlier, were not afraid to suggest that all are capable, at least in principle, of relating themselves to the divine Word in the power of the Spirit, although revelation and saving grace are necessary to accomplish this.

But when this line of thought threatens to become too triumphalist, supposing that mankind can grow beyond its dependence upon Jesus, a Schleiermacher or a Tillich is there to assert, within the framework of a totally "modern" theology, the indispensability of Christ and the impossibility of any such development beyond him, and saying it on the basis not of speculation but of the existential problem of man's guilt and incapacity in relation to God.

When one or the other of these strategies is tempted to be too narrowly Christian and make too many claims for a single historical heritage, the first group (Kant and the others) serves to remind them that real Christianity may be broader than the person of Christ and his specific influence in history, that what he actualizes and discloses within himself is relevant everywhere, and may be known, even actualized, at sundry times and in diverse manners before and apart from him.

What makes them all legitimate is that they have gained insight into three different aspects of the situation of man before God. The tradition stemming from Kant, which I have associated with the "first article," takes the perspective of the *beginning*—man's potentialities and his freedom for self-actualization, God's promise or demand. It remains *prospective*, always looking ahead; it cannot endure to hear of any claims that the ideal has become adequately embodied within human life, for it knows only how to deal with an ongoing process that recedes into an infinite future. The tradition stemming from Schleiermacher, associated with the "second article," takes its perspective from *historical enactments*—the partial and ambiguous achievements of men and women, their failures, and consequently their dependence upon redemptive events that have also been wrought out in the midst of human history. With Paul and Augustine and Luther, it practices a theology fitting to man *in pilgrimage*, confident that the resolution has already been offered, but also knowing that it remains outside oneself and can be appropriated only through struggle. The tradition stemming from Hegel, associated with the "third article," takes the perspective of the *eschaton* and sees the dawning of something that is final and satisfying even in the earthly present; although it may be prey to fanaticism or sentimentalism by claiming to see too much, it can usually make good its claim that something is there to be seen, some aspect of *fulfillment*, of *fruition*. We need all these perspectives, and there is no way to absorb one into another, because they have apprehended different points along the road from potentiality to actualization—or perhaps different aspects of the same point somewhere along that road.

Now if we are to begin extracting ourselves from the mental atmosphere of that classic era of German thought and eventually come out on the other side, we must begin looking at the conflicts among opposing schools, or sometimes, as the case may be, the internal tensions that show themselves even where there are common assumptions. Three areas come readily to mind, one of them concerning the overarching method, another concerning some basic metaphysical assumptions, and a third directly concerning the person of Jesus.

The problem of method that is pertinent here is the tension between the demands of *system* and the desire to affirm *freedom*. This is one of the celebrated issues raised by Kierkegaard, especially in *The Sickness unto Death*, the last part. Speculation, he says, by "comprehending" and thus "positing" sin within a system, makes it into mere negation and impotence. But sin is itself a "positing," infinitely potentiated because of its opposition to God; it remains a scandal, and all attempts at comprehending it will be self-contradictory, paradoxical. Therefore S.K. takes upon himself the Socratic task of preserving a God-fearing ignorance and wonder in this area where the human meets the divine.

But we should not forget, in this connection, the earlier and today more obscure figure of Julius Müller, whose life work was to intensify the awareness of sin and its implications.[43] Like Kierkegaard (who

43. His best-known work, of course, is *Die christliche Lehre von der Sünde*, first published in 1839 (volume I) and 1844 (revision of volume I, together with volume II), translated from the fifth German edition by William Urwick under the title *The Christian Doctrine of Sin* (Edinburgh: T. & T. Clark, 1848). But his earliest and in some ways best insights, coming from his student days, are generally overlooked because they are contained in a theological "romance" written by his close friend August Tholuck, *Die Lehre von der Sünde und vom Versöhner, oder Die wahre Weihe des Zweiflers* (Hamburg, 1825, and often reprinted);

owed much to *"der Sünden-Müller"*), he saw that sin and guilt are the decisive refutation of all pantheistic speculative systems; for if sin arises from human freedom (and our feeling of guilt assures us of this), then it cannot be made reasonable through some kind of demonstration of its necessity for the unfolding and eventual fulfillment of either God or man. Thus he opposed the speculations of Schelling and Hegel, and even the milder views of Kant and Schleiermacher on the origin of sin. His single-minded resistance to any conception of man that might diminish individual responsibility and make sin the outcome of an inevitable development led him ultimately to retrace the steps of Origen and, to the astonishment of his age, suppose a pre-temporal fall of each individual soul. But that was only a speculative conclusion of his own, based on a perception of the inadequacy of other treatments of evil and a desire to make the most of Kant's suggestion that radical evil is the work of "transcendental freedom," beyond all empirical influences. "The doctrine of monism may explain nature and the world," he says in a youthful letter preserved in the Tholuck volume, "it may dissolve spirits and annihilate space and time with its theories —but it does not know the diminuitive heart of man with its immense needs, and when it is injured it cannot heal it." If sin is taken seriously, it cannot be made "reasonable" in any way; it is unreasonable, a contradiction. That does not mean that it is in every sense impossible. If it were not possible it could not have become actual, and its possibility follows necessarily from finite freedom. But it should have remained a mere possibility. Its becoming an actuality is due to man alone, and God can permit it because he knows how to overcome it and use it in the service of his redeeming love.

When there is this kind of dramatic interaction between human freedom and divine freedom, it is impossible to take a speculative overview that would make either sin or the incarnation a phase of an organic development. For Müller, the only fixed point is to be found in God and his eternal ideas, equivalent with his ultimate purpose. Therefore in his thinking about the finite the stress falls upon God's goal of realizing his purpose in the kingdom of God, but the details of the

---

"Guido" is Tholuck himself, "Julius" is Müller—many of whose ideas are obviously preserved, perhaps literally, in the letters of "Julius." "Father Abraham," who appears briefly at the end, is Baron von Kottwitz, the guiding spirit of the pietistic circle in Berlin which influenced many budding theologians of that era.

movement toward that consummation are contingent events based upon God's knowledge of free human acts and his own response to them in the light of his purpose.[44] Such an insistence upon the freedom of man and the openness of the universe, going against the grain of much of the thought contemporaneous with him, may get a better response in our own day. In any event we should take note of it as an alternative to the common tendency of speculative theologians to make sin one phase in a pattern of development or even to find a "supralapsarian" rationale for the incarnation and the entire history of salvation.

The second problem is like unto the first, but this time it concerns a substantive metaphysical question, the relation of *God* to the *world*, and specifically to *man*. Baur and Strauss exposed it most dramatically when they pointed out the difficulty, if not the impossibility, of showing how the ideal can be embedded in a single individual. Their contribution is all the more valuable because their objection arises from the consistent application of a principle they shared with those they criticized; thus they exposed, in part knowingly, in part unwittingly, the unfortunate consequences of one of the most widely held assumptions of their era. The assumption I have in mind is that the infinite can somehow be embodied in and channeled through the finite. Schelling's philosophy is a prime instance of this; Hegel's also, though in a different way. But they are not alone; the tendency was already present in the Swabian pietism out of which they both came, and it is to be found in thinkers of the generation following them who agreed only partially with their systems. As a consequence the age was strongly tempted to overestimate the constructive potentialities of human life, and the clue is always an overinflated, excessively edifying language. Evidence for this accusation is abundant: the tendency to see man's social and cultural fulfillment in the Europe of their day, or, if not that, just beyond the next reform or revolution; the use of grandiose language to describe the human spirit, its qualities, and its contents; and, as though in answer to the need to find ultimate justification for these tendencies, the interest in the earthly Jesus as the perfection of human life, a kind of guarantee that eternity can quite properly be focused upon time and expend its wealth upon it.

Baur and Strauss shared that assumption, but they had the good

---

44. *The Christian Doctrine of Sin*, II, 217–18.

sense to recognize that, on *these* terms, it is absurd to suppose that everything can be poured into the one earthly figure of Jesus of Nazareth, and that everything must instead be diffused through the whole of human history. If history is the manifestation of the infinite in the finite, then that manifestation can never be completed within the finite. Their objection was not unanswerable—the Hegelians could still argue that Jesus' permanent uniqueness lay in disclosing to others their true nature and destiny, and those who were more or less in the succession from Schleiermacher could argue that it lay in his being the organizing center of the Church in which the divine dwells communally. But rather than gloating at their success in refuting Strauss, they might better have reflected on the problem he raised.

How, indeed, can the infinite be focused in the finite, how can an unconditioned ideal be instantiated in a historic individual? Strange though it may seem, this question was not often asked, whether because of the greater attraction of sheer speculation, or because of the continuing power of the orthodox belief that Jesus in fact fulfilled those specifications and an unwillingness to investigate the matter too closely, or because of an imperfect awareness of the difficulties that would have to be faced as a result of historical study of Jesus' life and times. In any event, the common assumption of the age was that the infinite is expressed in and channeled through the finite; but the debates of that era suggest that this may be a heavier load than the finite can bear. Let us examine the problem at somewhat greater length.

There is no intrinsic difficulty in supposing that the finite somehow reflects or participates in God's perfections. But the question is how these perfections—or an unconditional "ideal" for human life that is based in them—can be adequately realized within the finite. If we are looking for that realization in the form of qualities or other attributes that "inhere" in finite things, including human life, then we must be disappointed, for they will remain other than God and less than God. But when it comes to subjectivity, to "intentionality"—dispositions, desires, hopes, beliefs, knowledge—there *is* a capacity for the infinite, for the reason that the human subject need only be related to, directed toward, referred to the infinite in all its otherness from the self, and no inflated claims need be made concerning the inherent, analyzable qualities of the human being in question.

This is a point that was recognized often enough during the period we have been concerned with—by Kant, Hegel, Kierkegaard, the Ritschlians; strange bedfellows though they may be, they all knew the subjective character of man's relation to the infinite. But the spirit of the age overcame most of their contemporaries; they wanted to see the eternal made manifest in time, and to have objective guarantees—whether speculative, dogmatic, or historical—about it.

This brings us to the third problem, how to conceive *the earthly Jesus and his relation to God*. The historians and the theologians of the age have turned out to be especially vulnerable at this point. The Lutherans among them concentrated upon speculative deductions of the God-man; the Reformed looked to the human character of Jesus, basing their assertions upon the "impression" he made on his immediate associates or the historical information they could glean from the New Testament.[45] The Reformed theologians especially—Schleiermacher, Ullmann, and Rothe are the major names here—were notably guilty of trivialization, looking to the "moral perfection" of Jesus and attempting to demonstrate it historically.[46] The result was an incredibly sentimental and overwrought portrait of Jesus which might easily lie behind the banalities of popular religious art and the "creeping Jesus" satirized in the radical labor movement—to say nothing of the sickly, withdrawn, infantile figure dissected by Nietzsche and his followers.

We have since learned the impossibility and illegitimacy of such attempts to gain objective certainty about the assertions that are made about the earthly figure of Jesus. This is not to say that speculation, or doctrine, or historical investigation is impossible; all of them can go on,

45. This is pointed out quite effectively in Holte's *Die Vermittlungstheologie*, pp. 125–27.
46. The classic work of that era is Carl Ullmann, *Die Sündlosigkeit Jesu. Eine apologetische Betrachtung*, which reached at least seven editions during the author's lifetime and was translated by Sophia Taylor under the title *The Sinlessness of Jesus, An Evidence for Christianity* (Edinburgh: T. & T. Clark, 1882). It had begun as an article, entitled "Die Unsündlichkeit Jesu. Eine apologetische Betrachtung," in *Theologische Studien und Kritiken*, I (1828): 1–83, and was progressively expanded through controversy and further investigation. Although it is a skillful presentation of the archetype Christology, it is marred by a major flaw, its naive attempt to prove all of this by historical means—something that greater thinkers of his time would not even have tried. See also the christological passages in Richard Rothe's *Stille Stunden*, edited and published by Nippold in 1872 from Rothe's notebooks (translated under the title *Still Hours* by Jane T. Stoddart [New York: Funk and Wagnalls, 1895]).

and their paths may well converge. But speculation will yield only possibilities, not actualities; historical study, although it can undoubtedly uncover many facts, cannot by itself answer the kinds of questions that are most important; and faith, although it may answer these questions, cannot answer them with objective certainty.

In order to set before our sights the full extent of the problem, let us recall Jesus' deep immersion in the world of his day, the timely but also dated vocabulary he used, the localized contacts he had, the limited impact of his teachings and his actions. But beyond that, let us notice as well the difficulty of making a case for his sinlessness, certainly one of the crucial elements of his "archetypal" function. Ready at hand is one of the most recent and most forthright statements, by Gordon Kaufman:

> But according to the record Jesus did not, e.g., in a moralistic way, refrain from all peccadilloes or always hold his temper (cf. the cleansing of the temple, Mark 11:15ff.), nor did he always speak kindly and without sarcasm (cf. the denunciation of the Pharisees, Matthew 23). Neither was he perfect in more existentialist terms: never anxious or worried about himself or his fate (cf. the Gethsemane scene, Mark 14:32ff.), never tempted—and thus never tending—to seek fulfillment of his own desires instead of God's (cf. the temptation stories, Matt. 4:1ff., Luke 4:1ff., and the Gethsemane scene), never so frustrated and despairing as to doubt whether God was with him at all. . . .[47]

And he quotes from Karl Barth's *Romans*:

> Judged by the record of what he did and omitted to do, his sinlessness can be as easily denied as ours can, more easily, in fact, than the sinlessness of those good and pure and pious people who move about in our midst. And, indeed, his matter-of-fact contemporaries—who did not know what we think (!) we know—quite openly denied it.[48]

Can we be sure that Jesus was never implicated, at least indirectly, in sin, for example, by "purchasing a pair of sandals from a caravan not knowing that they were stolen property or produced with sweated labor in Baghdad"?[49] What about those more ambiguous matters,

47. *Systematic Theology: A Historicist Perspective* (New York: Charles Scribner's Sons, 1968), pp. 447–49, n. 12.
48. *The Epistle to the Romans*, translated from the sixth edition by Edwyn C. Hoskyns (Oxford: Oxford University Press, 1933), p. 279.
49. John Stewart Lawton, *Conflict in Christology: A Study of British and Ameri-*

about which the young Hegel, and in our own day writers like Camus and Kazantzakis, have agonized, legitimately if sometimes histrionically—his setting himself apart from his own people, his renunciation of vital human urges, his issuing demands that anyone could predict would not be met, his intensifying of tensions, his being a "stone of stumbling"? It is impossible to speak, in the fashion of Schleiermacher and Ullmann and Rothe, of the "beauty of his personality" and then suppose that his archetypal function will thereby stand out clearly.

Now there is one way of dealing with the problem that has been popular among theologians in the recent past: to circumvent it by first pleading the uncertainty of the historical evidence and then avowing nothing more than an expression of one's own belief about Jesus or one's own relation to him. They are right in recognizing the historical difficulties, and they are also right in stressing that Jesus must be described in terms of his function in relation to others and his meaning for their own lives—this is, indeed, a salutary influence that the archetype Christology has had upon modern theological reflection. But when all of these points are granted, still we are not kept from trying to devise, on the basis of whatever guidelines we can derive from reason, faith, or history, a conceptual framework for at least *possible* assertions about his life as it really was, even though we must always defer to the future findings of historical scholarship when it comes to filling in many of the important details.

The notion of the ideal archetype (and its precise content, as well as its provenance, may for the moment be left open) is helpful because it supplies a norm and goal applicable to all persons, even when all of them have failed to respond to it. Thus it indicates the kind of relevance Jesus could have to others, a connection "mediated" (in the Hegelian sense) through a universal demand and norm and goal. It is also helpful because it suggests a way in which Jesus, in all his finitude, can be linked to the ideal, precisely as ideal, without seeking to make it into an earthly actuality prematurely. This can be done by going beyond the external perspective of the objective observer and saying something, at least in a general form, about Jesus' inward life, for the finite can be opened out toward the infinite in and through the

---

can Christology from 1889 to 1914 (London: Society for Promoting Christian Knowledge, 1947), p. 110.

medium of mind and will, whereas it is impossible to suppose that the infinite can become, in some strict sense, a finite individual. We must resolutely say that the human remains less than the divine, although it can envisage the divine through its subjectivity.

Such a perspective enables us to give a place to a genuine human development in Jesus, even to a process of development that is conditioned by circumstances. It also enables us to avoid making assertions about Jesus' sinlessness that are based upon sentimental criteria or assume that his inner life was insulated from all threat and temptation. Sinlessness need not consist in a set of "qualities" inherent in him, nor in an unthreatened "state," as it seems to be in Schleiermacher's Christology; it might better be understood as a constantly renewed and developing enactment in the face of real temptations, as many thinkers even in Schleiermacher's own age saw.[50] Then it would not be the guaranteed absence of all acts that might scandalize others and be termed "sins"; nor would it be an unclouded innocence of inducements toward "sin," that is, a central orientation of rebelliousness or forgetfulness toward God; it would be, instead of these mere negations, an overcoming of the negative possibility of sin through responsible and responsive action in relation to both God and men.

Such a perspective enables us to take into account, finally, the breadth of vision that undeniably belongs to the Jesus of the Gospels and of critical historical research, for his life opens out upon God the Father of all, and upon the hoped-for kingdom of God, and upon the whole of humanity. Ritschl was perhaps the first theologian to recognize this and take it seriously when he focused attention on Jesus' vocation or personal aim and suggested that it was identical with God's own purpose of actualizing his kingship over all of mankind and of declaring forgiveness in order to bring men back into his company.[51]

---

50. Mention should be made of Kant's *Religion*, pp. 57–58 (*AA*, VI, 63–64); Ullmann's "Unsündlichkeit," pp. 10–11 (*Sündlosigkeit*, 7th edition, pp. 28–29); Baur's *DM*, III, 966; and Dorner's *Development*, pp. 256–57. Even closer to the mark are those thinkers in the line of Menken and Irving (note 23 above) who insisted upon Christ's assumption of "sinful flesh" and the overcoming of its inclinations in the power of the Holy Spirit.

51. Albrecht Ritschl, *The Christian Doctrine of Justification and Reconciliation*, III (Edinburgh: T. & T. Clark, 1902), 445–52; cf. Wolfhart Pannenberg, *Jesus—God and Man*, trans. Lewis L. Wilkens and Duane A. Priebe (Philadelphia: Westminster Press, 1968), pp. 191–211, 324–64, and his acknowledgment of the similarities with Ritschl on p. 194 and elsewhere.

The necessity of taking some such perspective has been underlined by subsequent studies in the Gospels, which have shown how large a part the proclamation of the kingdom played in Jesus' teachings—and in his depiction of his own role.

It is still a matter of controversy among the scholars in what sense the kingdom was proclaimed as "coming" and in what sense it was made "present" in his own activity. Many would argue that the kingdom as such was still to come, and was present only in his "speaking with authority," only in his offering the kingdom, as the anticipated content of his present proclamation, to those who would hear and respond; others would argue that the kingdom was somehow inaugurated, already dawning, in the activity of Jesus and that this is attested by the overtones of fulfillment and renewal that are so frequent in his message, and by the suggestions that the eschatological gift of the Spirit is being given, first in him and then in his followers, even though the further growth and complete fruition of the kingdom remains in the future. Here we have, if you will, a conflict between a "first article" and a "third article" perspective. There have been those who would even give an answer in terms of the "second article," asserting that the way to the kingdom—certainly in the early Church, perhaps in the message of Jesus himself—goes only through cross and resurrection, humiliation and exaltation. It might be, therefore, that the kingdom of God cannot be understood theologically, or even historically (that is, in the message of Jesus), without some combination or interpenetration of these three aspects.

In any event it is clear that Jesus cannot be understood solely as the fulfillment of an ideal, since he is also the proclaimer of the coming kingdom, and to it he devotes his attention, his energies, and his life. Thus we must add to the archetypal ideal of individual commitment, which somehow hovers over the human race from its beginning, the further goal or ideal of the kingdom of God (though the kingdom may well be, as Kant suggested, the full unfolding of all the implications of the ideal). Even if the original ideal is in some sense fulfilled by Jesus, the movement of human history is not slowed down when it reaches him but is, if anything, accelerated toward the realization of the kingdom in—or at least for—all people. Image of God, Messiah, kingdom of God—these are the foci of concern in the New Testament. Although they can interpenetrate, none of them can be collapsed into another, for they are held apart by the tensions in the historical process. A gap remains between demand and response, promise and fulfillment. A struggle continues between the Messiah and the corporate life of humanity, between Spirit and flesh, even while the first fruits of the kingdom can be recognized and enjoyed. A single schema of interpretation simply cannot be rich enough or complex enough to say all that needs to be said, and the different dimensions of man's relation to God must be affirmed together.

Our critical evaluation of the assumptions held by most of the thinkers of that earlier age will perhaps bring us out into the freer, more open atmosphere of the twentieth-century view of the world, radically pluralistic, subject to uncertainty, but for that reason also more susceptible of new possibilities. With such a view of the world man senses his own freedom with a greater intensity, anxiety-producing though it may be, and will be inclined to hear the divine call (if, indeed, he hears it at all) in terms of a purpose whose execution is stretched out over a long and fitful process of change and whose resolution is to be found only at the end, and even then perhaps only in the form of judgment and separation.

Enough has been said about the theory of the ideal in classical German philosophy to indicate that those men themselves knew that it was a philosophical version of the notion of purpose, and they were enough influenced by traditional theism to set their discussion within the context of God's purposes in creation and the history of the human race. Their talk about the ideal can be brought back without distortion into a more biblical and theological framework of meaning by speaking forthrightly, with Karl Barth and others, of God's covenant and its communication, or with Karl Rahner of God's self-impartation to man. Kant himself, influenced by the obscure Calvinist Stapfer, spoke of the ideal of a humanity pleasing to God as the essential content of God's "decree" in creation. The Reformed theologian Schleiermacher completed Kant's work by setting everything under a single eternal decree, taking account of man's slow development and centering all God's purposes on a redemption which would be simultaneously a new creation in Christ. Hegel's theory of the "idea" makes of it a concept whose real content, whose fulfillability, is guaranteed first of all by the attitude taken up within the divine life. So with men like Barth and Rahner the classical German philosophy, and the theology arising from it, have not been disowned but have been conducted, so to speak, back to their own home, not always gladly, to be sure, but with an undeniable shock of recognition. Let us turn, then, to an explicit discussion of this contemporary phase of the problem.

CHAPTER III

Christology and the Evolutionary Understanding of the World

We have come to the point of affirming some crucial elements of the theologies of Karl Barth and Karl Rahner, without doubt the two major theologians of recent years. For the biblical message can be drawn together into a unity with the notion of covenant, God's self-committal or self-impartation to men, establishing the comprehensive situation in which they find themselves and to which they must respond, favorably or not. This covenant supplies an eminently appropriate framework within which to speak of man's original potentialities, his estrangement from his proper destiny, the process of salvation, and his movement toward the ultimate fulfillment. Into this framework we can insert many of the particular insights arrived at by patristic and medieval and modern theologians.

But we have also seen that the Christocentrism of Barth and Rahner is not a necessary consequence of an emphasis on the covenant as the framework of all God's dealings with man. The assumption of most New Testament and patristic writers was that the incarnation of the Logos in a single human life is not necessary, or even fitting, except as a result of the contingent fact of human sin; and the new line of reflection inaugurated in the classic period of German philosophy serves to reinforce that same conclusion. It now remains to clinch the argument by looking into the problem of God's relation to the world and his purposes for it.

I. The Theological Implications of Evolution

We have already seen that Christocentrism, without necessarily diminishing the genuineness and even the momentousness of freedom in human history, at least nullifies the element of contingency and risk by introducing the incarnation as a guarantee of the success of the human enterprise from the beginning; with all contingencies prepared for, God cautiously hedges his bets and takes no chances. But it is precisely this that the traditional theologians denied. They held that the decree of incarnation followed upon God's foreknowledge of man's actually sinning, and they said this even at the cost of perfect consistency with their views on the timelessness of God's knowing and willing. But they were prepared to take the risk, I suspect, because they were committed less to a certain theory of eternity than to the biblical understanding of human life as a drama in which freedom and historical occurrence play a genuine role and there is a constant interaction between divine and human activity.

The problem is this: When one says that God knows all moments of time in a single, undivided, simultaneous act, which is required by the theory, it is impossible to think of God first creating man, then knowing his free acts, then willing further measures to counteract man's sin, for there would be three (or at the very least two) acts *in succession*, and that would be enough to make God's mental acts temporal rather than eternal. There are two possible ways to avoid the difficulty, but they pose an uncomfortable dilemma. Either give primacy to God's knowledge, as, for example, Boethius does (*De consolatione philosophiae*, V, prosa 6), but then God will become an eternally staring eye, timelessly knowing men's free acts but unable to react to them lest he forfeit his timelessness; or give primacy to God's willing, as Aquinas and Calvin and Leibniz do, but then God must bear exclusive responsibility for the choice of this particular world-order, and everything in it, out of the rich variety of human worlds, and human freedom becomes illusory, or at best the playing out of a decision already made by God. I am not saying that the doctrine of the timelessness of God's mental acts is meaningless or self-contradictory (although it may be that as well), only that it has implications that are unacceptable to a biblically oriented theology and must therefore be modified.

Lest this seem to be an alarming abandonment of a treasured doctrine, let me add that this affirmation of a temporal succession in God's experience does not imply a denial of his transcendence over the divisiveness that time has for us; rather it points us toward its more precise meaning. First, he has full knowledge of what is ideally possible (knowledge by "simple understanding" in the language of the scholastics), the kinds of formal structures and ordered changes that could be realized in the world. Second, he has perfect knowledge of all that actually occurs (knowledge by "vision" in the language of the scholastics), and, furthermore, when it perishes he does not lose hold on it through a failure of memory. Third, he has knowledge of the potentialities that are latent in the actual world at any given time, what it is capable of accomplishing now, what can grow out of it in the more or less distant future, what would occur under varying circumstances (what the Molinists called a "middle" kind of knowledge between the other two, the knowledge of "futuribles"). Thus God is not subject to temporality in a tragic way, as man is, suffering loss through the passage of time, anxious about the future because of ignorance of present factors or inability to anticipate new possibilities. But while his transcendance of temporal succession far surpasses anything man is capable of, it is not totally unlike man's own transcendence of succession through memory and anticipation, as Augustine saw when in the eleventh book of the *Confessions* he made human experience a partial model for what he wanted to say about God's eternity.

But the problems of dealing today with God and his purposes do not concern only this question of the timelessness or temporality of God's knowing and willing. Karl Barth, for example, who is quite ready to affirm a temporal interaction between God and man, holds nonetheless that the person of Jesus Christ is the one event which is *not* contingent upon human willing but was decided by God from eternity as the fulfillment of his covenant and thus would have occurred even if all other events had gone differently.[1] Even more generally, there seems to be, among theologians who have attempted to take seriously the evolutionary understanding of the world, an almost uniform tendency to view its long-term development toward man, and then man's long-term improvement in social and cultural and religious life, as a direct confirmation of the traditional conception of God's purposiveness, often with the incarnation as the preestablished goal. Pierre Teilhard de Chardin (especially in his 1924 essay, "Mon Univers"[2]) and Karl Rahner (espe-

---

1. *CD*, IV/1, 46–47.
2. *Oeuvres*, IX (Paris: Éditions du Seuil, 1965), 63–114; translated in the volume *Science and Christ* (New York: Harper & Row, 1968), pp. 37–84. For an uncriti-

cially in his essay "Christology within an Evolutionary View of the World"[3]) view the incarnation as the full and definitive fruition, always intended, of the long process of God's impartation of himself to the world and his union of the world to himself. In another vein, using not a participationist metaphysic but the vocabulary of personal agency,[4] Gordon Kaufman has recently been interpreting the unbroken web of interrelated occurrences, the "unitary evolutionary process," as the expression of a "single all-encompassing act of God" which ties together these seemingly disparate occurrences, indeed, is an "act" only when taken as a whole, not in its details, where there may be tragic dissonances.[5] This, I suggest, not only swallows up the parts into the whole, making their subjective desires and frustrations of no account, or of only infinitesimal value; it makes the finite process in all its unsatisfying details equivalent with God's "act." It is, in short, a re-issue of the theology of the Stoics, of Spinoza, and of Schleiermacher, and while it may be tenable, it is neither a new contribution from the evolutionary perspective on the world nor the most satisfactory version of the biblical understanding of God.

Theologians have often talked glibly about the evolutionary perspective and its consequences for theology when they have actually done no more than make some observations about the chronological sequence of evolution and then suppose that it indicates a slow but steady movement of all things toward Christ and the eschaton. What must be done first, however, is to consider the character of the evolving universe, as best it can be understood from present knowledge, and then to ask what its consequences are for theology.

It is not merely that we must now take seriously the dimension of time and acknowledge the slowness with which the present stock of

cally admiring presentation of Teilhard's Christocentrism, see Christopher Mooney, *Teilhard de Chardin and the Mystery of Christ* (New York: Harper & Row, 1966), and Donald Gray, *The One and the Many: Teilhard de Chardin's Vision of Unity* (New York: Herder & Herder, 1969), esp. chaps. 5 and 6.

3. *Theological Investigations,* V (London: Darton, Longman & Todd, 1966), 157–92.

4. The chief source for theologians has been John Macmurray, *The Self as Agent* (New York: Harper & Row, 1957).

5. See "On the Meaning of 'Act of God,'" *Harvard Theological Review,* XLI (1968): 175–201, esp. pp. 190–200; and, less explicitly, his *Systematic Theology,* chaps. 18–19.

chemical compounds, flora and fauna, has been assembled; not merely that the evolutionary process takes place step by step, that the outcome, however exalted it may be, is the product of occurrences that have taken place all along the way and continues to bear their stamp (as the morphology of the human body, for example, is conditioned by the many antecedent forms out of which it evolved). What is most shattering to our theological preconceptions—but it is so essential to the evolutionary theory, and so well verified, that it cannot be explained away—is that *chance*, by which I mean the random coincidence of independent chains of events, plays an irreducible role in the process. Chance or coincidence is a real and observable factor in finite occurrences: we see it when a man walking down the street to buy a loaf of bread is hit by a falling roof-tile (Spinoza's famous illustration), or when five people, each traveling to a destination of his own, happen to be crossing a suspension bridge when it collapses (the problem of Thornton Wilder's *The Bridge of San Luis Rey*), or when two automobiles collide—or narrowly miss each other (the problem of numerous popular speculations in theodicy). There is *no causal connection* between the chains of events; each physical object is acting according to its own influences, each human subject is acting according to his own intentions, but the confluence of events—or a narrow miss—may have momentous consequences.

It is similar in the evolution of living forms. The particular combination of chromosomes as two animals mate, the damaging of a gene by a cosmic ray that set out from a distant nova thousands or millions of years before, the capture of a particular animal by a predator, or its escape—these may have a permanent effect, either positive or negative, on the history of evolution. For the process of evolution is affected, first, by random combinations in the "gene-pool" of a population, then by the development and maturation of the resultant organisms, leading to "innumerable slight variations," as Darwin liked to put it, among the members of the population, and finally by the death or survival, escape or capture, mating or being rejected, of the particular individuals, in all of which even the slightest difference in genotype or phenotype may be crucial. Then the survivors pass on their genetic character to their descendants, and it is slowly amplified in generation after generation, and perhaps spreads throughout the population so that the species or a part of it eventually becomes another species.

Now if religious people are so eager to claim all of this for the wonders of God's creative activity, where are they going to point to it? In the mutations of the genetic structure? This is one common claim. But that is not chiefly a matter of mutation but of random combination according to statistical probabilities, and even mutation ultimately follows certain physical and chemical laws. Does God then manipulate the combination of genes? This is more likely to be a matter of coincidence, and if God is given credit for the successful combinations he must be blamed for the monstrous or abortive ones as well. Or does he somehow stage-manage the details of the process of natural selection? There again we would have to hold him directly responsible for all the horrors of predation, starvation, and disease as well as the constructive results. None of these attempts will work. We must acknowledge, then, the radically pluralistic character of the natural world, pervaded by conflict and coincidence as much as it is by balance and cooperation, and not attempt to inject divine influence where it cannot save the appearances but would if anything fly in the face of them.

But that does not mean that it is all up with the theistic explanation of the world. Finally, I think, we must join the broad consensus of those philosophers who have seriously confronted the problem in modern times—C. S. Peirce, Whitehead, Blondel, Teilhard, Rahner—and look for God's influence in the persistence and growth of order, of higher and more complex patterns of relationship and coordination, of broader and more inclusive activities, postulating that this influence consists not in manipulating, "from below," the random combinations that arise, but in sustaining whatever is viable and encouraging it to exert itself according to its highest potentialities, supplying, "from above," the unifying influence that gives coherence at many different levels to the jumble of occurrences.[6]

What this means is that God's influence is not to be understood on the model of human actions, which are, despite the role of intelligent purpose in them, the actions of bodies within the realm of spatio-tem-

6. Justification for this perspective can be found, *mutatis mutandis*, in Augustine, who differentiated between the "propagation" of the genetic code from one generation to the next and the "conformation" of the living being, and laid the stress upon the latter. (He believed, of course, that the genetic code for each species was created, once and for all, at the very beginning.) Therefore, he says, "those who copulate cannot generate a new being except as [God] creates ... for it is he who, through that action with which he works even now, causes the seeds to develop according to their numerical proportions. . . ." (*De civ. Dei*, XXII, 24)

poral interaction—that would be a "mythical" conception to which none of the great theologians of the past ever held—but as the sustaining, and urging on, and bringing to fruition those potentialities that are latent in things. His influence is felt and reflected differently in every kind of thing and at every level (*"pro suo modulo,"* as Augustine liked to put it).

God's influence need not be a blind and undifferentiated one, taken up in a different way by each thing merely because of its own receptivity; it can just as well be complexly structured and focused differently upon each thing, in keeping with its character and situation, in order to educe the best that is possible from it. This should not be surprising, for with the Einsteinian separation of events in space-time no causal event is exactly contemporaneous with its effect in another event. If every event has its own unique locus, isolated from other events on its own lonely summit, with the cone of interaction spreading out behind (all the influences upon it) and before (its potential scope of influence)—if the universe is basically pluralistic or "strung-along" rather than a "block universe," to use the suggestive language of William James—God's relation to events may be diversified, many-colored, appropriate to the variegated matrix of potentialities and the divergent interactions that could develop within it.[7]

7. This is, of course, a crucial element in Whitehead's view that God supplies an "initial aim" to each occasion in accordance with its own antecedents and his own evaluative grading of the possibilities, and I would regard these liberating consequences of relativity physics as far more important theologically than the perplexities which it raises for the understanding of God's mode of knowledge. But this latter problem has been the theme of an important discussion among Whiteheadians, and it is pertinent to what has been said earlier in the present chapter. The discussion began with John Wilcox, "A Question from Physics for Certain Theists," *Journal of Religion*, XL (1961): 293–300, which was answered by Lewis S. Ford, "Is Process Theism Compatible with Relativity Theory?" *Journal of Religion*, XLVIII (1968): 124–35. These articles, and especially another article by Ford, "Boethius and Whitehead on Time and Eternity," *International Philosophical Quarterly*, VIII (1968): 38–67, have now occasioned further reflections by Paul Fitzgerald, "Relativity Physics and the God of Process," *Process Studies*, II (1972): 251–76. Fitzgerald, after surveying several possible lines of approach to God's mode of knowledge in a relativistic universe, comes down favorably upon Ford's view that God experiences the total succession of events in a single "synoptic" act without the loss of any of them to the past, without any need for "recollection," since the awareness of them all remains vividly alive, without subsiding (Fitzgerald, p. 266; cf. Ford, "Boethius and Whitehead," pp. 50–51). Then he improves upon this suggestion and puts forward the possibility that God's *experiencing* of events is at the time and place of their occurrence, but that he has a *concomitant awareness* of them which is not at any physical standpoint and is non-temporal (pp. 268–70), although at the end he criticizes his own suggestion because of a number of other difficulties that this "non-temporal" awareness involves:

Add to this the evolutionary understanding of the growth of all physical and biological and social realities, and it becomes impossible to
suppose that the slow process of cosmic and biological evolution is
held together from God's side by an "external teleology" planned out in
advance, so that every occurrence is manipulated as a means toward
further developments, according to a prearranged sequence. If there is
anything we have learned about the world it is that the general pattern
of events is loosely textured and that their specific course has been
affected at every stage by random coincidences and spontaneous
actions. If there is to be any teleology at all, it must be compatible with
a highly pluralized state of affairs and the teleological aim at the start
can scarcely be more specific than for the fullest or best development
along each line of inheritance. This does not mean that every individual, and every tendency, will be an end in itself—sexual desire and
protective instincts, for example, have the biological function of preserving the population, and human intelligence and will can serve a

---

What has been determinative in this line of discussion, it seems to me, is not so
much the space-time problem of relativity physics as the desire to interpret Whitehead, in particular his view that God's life is not a "society" or "succession" of
occasions but is rather a single subjective experience in everlasting concrescence.
This Whiteheadian dogma, while it has its virtues (especially in showing how
God's experience, even though temporal, need not involve either the recollection of
a lost past or hope for an alien future), and is preferable to the alternative view
that God's life is fragmented into a whole society of "godlings," as Fitzgerald calls
these separate experiences, still has its shortcomings. Out of anxiety to keep the
unity of the divine life, both Ford and Fitzgerald fall into many of the same
difficulties that we have already pointed to in older doctrines of "eternity" or a
"single divine act," for insofar as it denies succession in God's acts it is unable to
give sufficient room for innovation in God's purposes.

It appears to me that we must differentiate between "succession" in the sense
that one act perishes and gives way to another (following the usual Whiteheadian
paradigm for the transition from one actual occasion to the next) and "succession"
in the sense of genuine innovation in the course of time, which is a matter of
making new decisions or projecting new aims and is fully compatible with the
retention of all completed experiences in their unfading freshness and immediacy.
The possibility of a differentiation of this sort has been overlooked in the Whiteheadian tradition, I suspect, for two reasons. One is a physicalist bias in Whitehead's philosophy such that, despite all his efforts to take subjective experience
seriously, he did not scrutinize it as persistently as he might. The other is that
Whitehead assumed that God has no other life than that which he has in relation
to the world process, and thus may have been overly anxious to maintain the unity
of God's life through the sheer feat of spanning all of time in a single act as the
"eros of the universe." Traditional Christian thought has been prepared, by contrast, to run the risk of using language that suggests a succession in God's acts, and
it may have been freed from Whitehead's anxiety by the Trinitarian doctrine,
which showed how God could have a fullness of life and self-relatedness within
himself and could therefore be free for spatial and temporal relatedness outside
himself.

wide variety of ends, real or ideal, beyond themselves; but it remains true even in these cases that the relation of means and ends is worked out and made good in isolated instances, always in terms of finite interactions, and is not imposed and manipulated from the outside.

If heresy-hunters in the scientific world have somehow failed to follow the argument, let me say that I do not have in mind what usually goes under the name of "internal teleology," namely, the vitalist thesis that the growth and improvement of living forms is the result of a striving on the part of some life-principle. That hypothesis is unnecessary to describe and account for the phenomena. All I mean is that physical things do have a tendency to persist in what they are, and that living beings have, beyond that, a tendency toward growth and self-preservation and responsiveness and mutual relationship. I am fully prepared to acknowledge that these are descriptive facts whose mechanisms can be traced by physics and chemistry, and whose rise in the first place can be explained simply as an emergence through natural selection. Even tendencies and desires can be dealt with as empirical facts of the natural world, as in the tradition of "ethical naturalism" springing from John Dewey and Ralph Barton Perry, which calls attention to the vital acts of valuing and selecting without finding itself compelled at any point to bow before inexplicable mysteries.[8]

But now let us examine the possibility that advantages which are often lumped together under the general designation of "survival value," or at least many of them—regularity, endurance, harmony, coordination, adaptability, aggressiveness, cleverness, responsiveness, mutual attraction and cooperation, inquisitiveness, self-transcendence —can also be viewed, from another perspective, as being grounded in God and "reflecting" or "participating in" his perfection, though always in a finite way, in some *mode* and to some *degree*, perhaps in an astounding fashion (the tiger as well as the lamb, the hyena as well as the tiger, and the intestinal parasite, too), in every case in keeping with the conditions imposed by finite existence, for if there are to be any finite reflections of God they must have a physical basis and make good their claims in a fair contest with other physical beings, within some set of concrete circumstances.

8. For a recent exploration of this tradition in relation to natural science see the various articles in the March, 1969, issue of *Zygon: Journal of Religion and Science*.

Immediately we confront a difficulty, however, for there are other kinds of survival value, such as camouflage, imitative markings, recognition codes, sexual coloration, and the like, which are a matter of external appearance rather than internal activity, depending as they do upon the perception and instinctual response of other beings, either by appealing to them directly or by evading them. Such cases serve to remind us that any satisfactory ontology of finite things must take fully into account their interrelationships, the way they are "mirrored" in one another; indeed, the emphasis probably falls on the perceptual discrimination or obtuseness of the *other* beings, not upon the beings with these traits. But such interrelationships can even be constitutive of the very origin and survival of species. For example, the flowering plants have evolved only in symbiosis with the bees and then the humming-birds, and their bright colors and fragrant aromas, however these may be perceived by the bees and hummingbirds, are "essential attributes" of such plants, attracting the visitors who have become indispensable for pollination and in turn supplying them nutrition. The most tangible instances of "survival value"—claws, teeth, hard shells, and the like —are, so to speak, a grosser and purely external case of interrelationship, having to do simply with physical and chemical qualities and their effects on other things; but these are more clearly "instrumental" to the life-processes and the total "way of life" of the organism.

If, in addition to all of this, we must also take into account the vast ecological systems within which living things find their place, an almost unmanageable complexity is introduced into any "ontology" of finite being. Still I would like to pursue the possibility that these unified activities of an organism—not only the more spontaneous ones but also those which are more responsive to other beings—can be considered as modes of participation in God.

It may help to move the argument forward if we make some distinctions which are usually missed, despite their being so crucial, among various meanings of the terms *function* and *value.* I have already spoken, for example, of "survival value," which denotes the various traits of an organism which enable it to endure and even prevail in the contest with other beings and the competition for scarce resources. These traits are said to have "value for" or to be "functional for" the survival of the organism or the reproduction of the species. This is a rather indirect kind of functionality, merely *de facto* and not involving any intrinsic link between trait and function, the same sort of relationship that is traced by sociologists when they speak of the social functions of, say, religious rituals which have no apparent social meaning. But we may also speak, secondly, of the function of parts or processes within the interacting physiological system of the organism: the heart "has the function of" pumping blood in response to certain endocrine or respiratory signals, just as a flywheel "has the function of" stabilizing a motor. Here we have in mind a direct contribution made by a part to the whole, and the language of function is a substitute for the teleological language that has often been used in this connection. And finally we can speak of the "functioning" (or not functioning) of the whole, or of a part of the whole. When we say that a motor is not "functioning," or that the visual system is not "functioning," we seem to presuppose that it should be "functioning *as*" a motor, or as a visual system, in certain patterns of action or response. This last, I suggest, is the meaning of function that finally counts, for what is most interesting and important about living beings is not simply the mutual adaptation of their parts but the integrated activity of the entity as a whole, or at least of its major systems; indeed, it is this, according to evolutionary theory, that enables them to pass the more tangible features of structure and physiology on to their descendants. Since the emphasis does fall here, we need make no great claims about the intrinsic constitution of the organism—it can be totally earth-born—but at the same time we can take seriously the possibility that, just as a word is what it is because of its "function" and not because of its bare components, there may be a similar transubstantiation as the organism and its physiological interrelations are seen to come to a focus in vital acts, even to be sustained by them and (when seen from an evolutionary perspective) to owe their very existence and character to them.

Since God's aim cannot consist in plotting out everything in advance (for the process is too open-textured, too unpredictable for that), it must consist instead in supporting the ensemble of things already actualized and, beyond that, in drawing them on toward higher achievements and new modes of interaction. This will not mean that God's aim is determined only on an ad hoc basis, moment by moment, for he knows the potentialities latent in the actual world, and he knows the fresh modes of participation in his own being that could arise within the finite. Therefore he can make all sorts of contingency plans, although their realization will be conditioned upon what actually happens. Even here, however, we may have to make allowance for a considerable degree of inventiveness on God's part. Is the subjective quality or feeling that we call "blue," for instance, an eternal idea in God's mind? Probably not, unless it can be shown to follow necessarily from the wave-lengths and neural processes involved, or from the possible modalities of consciousness. What is more likely is that it is a potentiality seized and exploited in the midst of the evolutionary process.[9]

But really the participationist scheme that I have been spelling out neutralizes any religious anxieties that might arise from these suggestions that God's knowing and willing of the future are not completely detailed in advance, for the thesis of a "structural" or "situational" teleology would be that God's own perfection is the basis and guarantee of progress, present and complete from the beginning. The entire process of evolution is, from this perspective, a moving into God—that is, a narrowing of the difference between God and the corporeal world with its dispersiveness and mutability, the world's becoming more like God and thus participating more and more in his perfect coherence and stability of life. The teleology is built into the structure of the total situation, God plus an open universe. The increasing likeness to God can be reached by many paths, and there need be no basic anxiety to find a single set of means and safeguard it at all costs.

The point may become clearer if we consider a familiar analogue in evolutionary theory, the phenomenon of "convergence." The eye is approximated to in many animal families with photoreceptors of various sorts, and it has developed fully as an image-forming receptor with lens and retina in two very different phyla, the Mollusca (especially the octopods) and the Chordata (above all the birds and mammals). Optically the mechanism is almost exactly the same, but the tissues from which the eyes develop in the embryo are different because in the course of evolution the two phyla were totally independent of each other.[10] Again, wings have evolved three times from the fore-

---

9. See, for example, the exploration of this problem in Newton P. Stallknecht, *Studies in the Philosophy of Creation, With Especial Reference to Bergson and Whitehead* (Princeton: Princeton University Press, 1934), which attempts to mediate between Bergson's non-rational *élan* and Whitehead's overly explicit "eternal objects."

10. George Gaylord Simpson, *The Meaning of Evolution: A Study of the History of Life and of Its Significance for Man* (New Haven: Yale University Press, 1949),

limbs of terrestrial vertebrates—in pterodactyls, in birds, and in bats—filling the same function, but developing from different combinations of bones because of the independent courses of evolution.[11] In less striking ways the fossil record is full of convergent forms: the marsupials of Australia and Tasmania developed into a variety of forms, analogous to the rodents, the carnivores, even the tree-climbing primates; and the extinct mammals of the South American past exhibit forms similar to camels, horses, carnivores, and the like, despite the lack of direct relationship with them.[12]

Now none of these cases requires for its explanation a divine "design" or a teleologically striving "life-principle." It is simply a process of natural selection, blindly utilizing the gene-pool that was available and the genetic combinations that arose in a random way within it. The reason for the convergence is that some common environmental demands are placed upon living organisms, and image-forming eyes, wings, herbivorous (or carnivorous) instincts and equipment, even the half-way measures leading up to them, will all make a difference to the survival of an organism in the contest among living forms. Thus the genetic and environmental conditions account for all the factors that influence the result. No additional divine influence, no divine planning in advance, are needed. The rise of higher forms and their convergence could come about simply because of the conditions furnished and the pressures exerted from below. That is enough for scientific purposes.

Yet we can legitimately raise further questions, philosophical ones, for there is a rise in the quality of life, there is "more being," as Teilhard put it, in the sense that there is an increase in the scope and subtlety of activity. As long as violence is not done to the scientifically explicable facts in the case it is legitimate to suggest that God is the enabling cause of this improvement or increase of being, the origin of these new modalities of activity, the ground of their coherence.

In the *Phaedo* (97C–98C) Socrates says that in his youth he had industriously studied the philosophers who investigated the processes of the natural world, and was totally captivated by their way of think-

---

pp. 168–76. Teilhard was also aware of it: cf. *The Phenomenon of Man* (New York: Harper & Row, 1959), pp. 125–26.

11. Ibid., p. 181.

12. Ibid., pp. 177–80.

ing (that is, to explain everything in terms of natural ingredients and processes) until he heard someone reading from a book by Anaxagoras in which it was said that Mind is the disposer and cause of all. Although Anaxagoras did not carry through with this insight, Socrates did, and conjectured that the physical elements and their interactions are, indeed, the "conditions" of things, but that the "cause" is Mind, which disposes everything in accordance with the absolute norm of goodness and beauty (so far as it is physically possible, of course). The distinction between "conditions" and "causes" is a good one, although perhaps the emphasis on Mind carries too much of a suggestion of anterior design and manipulation, and causation should be ascribed not only to God but also to the interacting and "looping" systems of the finite world itself.

A better version of the same insight, therefore, may be contained in Aquinas' quick sketch of the history of philosophy (*Summa Theologica*, I, q. 44, a. 2; *De potentia*, q. 3, a. 5). At first, he says, the "physical" philosophers asked about the origin of things *as individuals* (*"hoc ens"*) and explained it in terms of new groupings of matter. Then Plato and Aristotle asked about the origin of things *as substances*, that is, as members of a species (*"tale ens"*), and they answered *their* question in terms of form. Then others who are unnamed—perhaps the neo-Platonists, and certainly Avicenna—asked about the origin of things *as beings* (*"ens in quantum est ens"*), and *this* question could only be answered in terms of a universal creative principle.

Aquinas' way of putting the problem indicates more clearly that the outcome is not merely the result of insight into the evident features of the world, for our explanations will depend in large part upon the questions we ask, and we always have the privilege of refusing to ask the question about *being* or *actuality*, or of regarding it as illusory, or superfluous, or unanswerable. But wherever the question is taken seriously, it does seem to generate (if it did not even originate from) a concern about God; and even where the answer is finally No, as in a Jean-Paul Sartre, that same concern is still present. The point, then, is that the influence of "conditions"—the potentialities and the materials that are supplied, the pressures that are exerted, the challenges that are posed—and even of finite "causes" may be all-comprehensive, determining what can and cannot be accomplished, and yet not constitute a sufficient explanation of another aspect of the emergent beings, their unity and stability, their openness to other beings, their striving beyond themselves.

What we are dealing with here is the coordinating and unifying activity that draws a multiplicity of physical occurrences and interrelationships into a single life or being. It is what Leibniz called the "dominant monad" or *vinculum substantiale,* Blondel the synthesizing activity through which a plurality of components is bound together,[13] Teilhard "creative union,"[14] Rahner the self-transcendence of the finite by which a new dimension of being establishes itself.[15] It is not that some new "stuff" is infused from above, for the potentiality comes entirely from below, from the components assembled out of the familiar world of matter and energy in such a way as to form the vehicle for new, increasingly unified and yet increasingly flexible acts. We should be willing to concede that the activities of living organisms are explicable on cybernetic or information-processing models, in terms of electrical fields, binary switches, feedback loops, and the like, already familiar both in electronic computers and in the nervous system; that would only be consistent with what has been said about "conditions." We should even be willing to concede—indeed, affirm—with spirits like Nietzsche or Sartre that it is a self-creation of sorts, a positing, from below, of new activities, new meanings, new being; nothing ventured, nothing gained, for this is the way life grows. Indeed, we do not have the right to speak of divine influence until we are sure we have taken hold of finite actuality in its fullness.

Yet we can also ask a philosophical or religious question, quite different from the scientific question, focusing our attention upon these new levels of unified activity that are achieved by a complex, coordinated organism. For it is, after all, the lived unity of a being and the coherence of its acts that finally count in its own course of life and in its competition with other beings. Since these new levels have come into being *ex nihilo* (leaving aside their material components and pre-

---

13. *Une énigme historique: Le 'vinculum substantiale' d'après Leibniz et l'ébauche d'un réalisme supérieur* (Bibliothèque des archives de philosophie; Paris: Beauchesne, 1930), and especially the illustration given in the appendix.

14. "Mon Univers," *Oeuvres,* IX, 72–75, translated in *Science and Christ,* pp. 44–47.

15. *Hominisation: The Evolutionary Origin of Man as a Theological Problem* (London: Herder, 1965), pp. 80–93; "Christology within an Evolutionary View of the World," *Theological Investigations,* V: 162–67.

conditions, the activities themselves are radically new), we can and must ask whether they have arisen solely through the process and its interactions, or are somehow educed by God as they mount to intensified degrees of activity and relationship. The question can be asked in several different ways, each of which will suggest a slightly different modality of divine influence. It may be asked in terms of the sheer *"thatness"* of these radically contingent levels of activity. This is the perspective of the Thomistic "five ways," pointing toward God as "Being itself." Or it may be refined and be phrased more analytically in terms of the *order* they evince—not their physical structure as such, but the functioning of all the parts and especially the complex interaction of these functions. This perspective may yet show the way toward a new, more empirically based "Platonism" which focuses its attention upon the interacting and developing set of functional relationships whose vehicle is the complex structure of the physical organism.[16] The question may be asked, finally, in terms of the quasi-voluntaristic *unification* of these many interrelationships into focused acts. Here there will be an emphasis, above all, upon God as will, sustaining the activities of each being from within itself, as in Blondel or Teilhard. I suspect that all three perspectives will have to be taken seriously, since each seizes upon a different aspect of the same phenomenon, emergent activity.

All of this, it will be recalled, has been by way of explicating the assertion, made a few pages back, that the guarantee of evolutionary progress is not a detailed planning and manipulating but simply the presence of God to the matrix of potentialities that makes up our evolving world. The point for the theological controversy in which we are engaged is that it has become impossible to hold to a Christocentric, even an anthropocentric view of the world in the strict sense. We cannot say that man, as *this particular* species, the featherless biped with five-digited limbs, called *Homo sapiens*, is the goal of creation, or that Christ, as the presence of the Word in one human life, is the goal and center of all things. The process is more indeterminate than that,

---

16. I am thinking not of the problems dealt with by Ludwig von Bertalanffy, Walter Elsasser, Michael Polanyi, and their critics, who are concerned with the relation between physical structures or processes and the uniquely biological processes of the total organism, but rather of the Continental movement exemplified especially by Jean Piaget and traced in his *Structuralism* (New York: Basic Books, 1970; reprinted Harper Torchbooks, 1971), for it recognizes the importance of the acts themselves and then goes about tracing their interrelations and development.

for there are many things that might have happened differently along the line of descent leading to man, and at every stage God can be thought to have only a limited range of specific goals in view, based on what *could* happen, given the potentialities then existing.

Yet the process is not so hazardous as this makes it appear. Even though the exact forms of life are affected by circumstance and coincidence, there is still the phenomenon of convergence: given a challenge to meet, life eventually meets it under the terms of the challenge, and the successful response, especially if it leads to a higher form and opens up further possibilities, can be said to be grounded in God and even led by his wisdom. Therefore if intelligence had not arisen along the line leading to man, the featherless biped, it might have arisen along some other path of inheritance, morphologically different but functionally the same (and the biologists are able to specify with increasing precision the range of conditions under which this could happen). Indeed, if we make the necessary qualifications we can even say that man—as the actually existing form of intelligent and free life —is the goal of the process in our world, for intelligence and freedom are obviously at the summit of biological values, enabling an organism to survive and adapt itself to an indefinite variety of environments, and it is also the beginning of a new mode of life, concerned with ideal values consciously known and freely pursued. It is thus the mode of life that most nearly approximates to God's own, and it is even capable of union with God through knowledge and love. Therefore if God's general aim is to bring the world to its highest perfection, then that aim will be realized along the path or paths which in fact lead toward finite intelligence and freedom, and then toward social cooperation, cultural and intellectual activity, and religious dedication. But we would still not be able to say that Christ is the antecedent goal of the process, whether considered as a member of the human race or as the Word incarnate. The theological position that is more in keeping with the openness and contingency of the universe is what we have seen to be the traditional one, that the office of the Messiah is exercised only because of sin, and even through a triple contingency—human sin, the decision of God, and the obedience of faithful men and women in Israel.[17]

17. This last is at least one part of the meaning of the Catholic Church's attentiveness to the Annunciation and Mary's *fiat* (I would refer the reader especially to

All of this enables us, by the way, to give a quick answer, which is all that is needed, to the problem of "space theology" that has been aired in the popular press in recent years. Now that we know that the universe has so many galaxies, with so many stars capable of having planets which would support life, it is a statistical certainty that there are intelligent beings elsewhere, perhaps on millions of planets, most of them kept from communicating with each other by the vast spaces between them.[18] It becomes quixotic or narcissistic to think that our earth, or the Christ who appears on it, is *the* goal and center of the entire universe. There must be many centers, at different times, and in each of them the emergence and enhancement of intelligent life can be called the goal. The morphological variety among such beings is of course inconceivable, as is the variety of their cultural and religious histories. The only appropriate way to think about them theologically, in the absence of any information, is to hold open *all* the contingencies —sinlessness, sometimes naive and sometimes open-eyed; spiritual corruption, sometimes mild in its effects and sometimes drastic; salvation without a redeemer; a redeemer, sometimes rejected and sometimes not; millennial perfection; continued ambiguity; abysmal and satanic failure. All that can be asserted with confidence is a tendency—sometimes fulfilled, sometimes not—to converge toward union with the God who is present everywhere in all his perfection.

Now we are in a position to diagnose the insights and the excesses of the chief "Christocentrists" in modern theology—Blondel, Teilhard, Barth, Rahner—and to engage in *diairesis*, separating their successes from their failures. All of them are aware of the historical dimension, the law of gradual growth, the indispensable role of finite accomplishment, the reality of human decision. Many of the statements I have been making are of course based upon their thought. Yet all of them view the incarnation (together with its effects in the life of the human race) as the goal of the entire process, the center upon which all else is focused. Indeed, they assume, with invincible certitude, that an evolutionary understanding of the world and belief in the incarnation

---

chapter 8 of *Lumen gentium*, Vatican II's dogmatic constitution on the Church), and much of it can be extended backward into Israel and forward into the Church.
18. The classics appear to be Harlow Shapley, *Of Stars and Men: The Human Response to an Expanding Universe* (Boston: Beacon Press, 1958), and I. S. Shklovskii and Carl Sagan, *Intelligent Life in the Universe* (San Francisco: Holden-Day, 1966).

belong together, that the affirmation of the one somehow entails affirmation of the other, with belief in the incarnation as senior partner. For them everything is held together by Christology; Christ must permeate all things.

Blondel speaks of *"panchristisme,"* which means that the ultimate context and meaning of all things, individually and collectively, is the incarnate Christ, who joins finitude to infinitude and gives to finite experience (its subjectivity and privacy, its relativities, its play of colors and sounds which are mere "secondary qualities" from an objective standpoint) a status for God himself, as part of his *own* experience.[19] Barth and Rahner do not engage in that sort of speculation, but they have another of their own: that God's one comprehensive decision is to impart himself to that which is other than himself, and that the creation of man, and the entire process leading up to man, even the cosmos itself, play a role in God's purposes only because they are required by the incarnation as a necessary though not sufficient condition of its occurring at all. They seem to think, furthermore, that because of this self-impartation the whole world is different from what it might otherwise have been.

But according to some classical principles of metaphysics, which they are only too glad to adopt in other connections, God's influence upon the world must at every stage be in accordance with its own potentialities and modes of action. Although we have argued that his influence need not be an undifferentiated one, channeled solely by the receptivity of each individual thing, but could be given a bias in one direction or another in keeping with his purposes, the rule would still hold: God's purposes are translated into finite change and growth only in the mode and to the degree that things are susceptible of them, and until we get to the human mind there is no possibility at all of their envisaging distant goals. We have already seen that it is impossible for other reasons to argue that earlier stages of the process are "means," in the strict sense, to the end (they are, of course, stages along the way, a de facto preparation for what finally results), since the process is so open and contingent as to frustrate any such attempt to control it, even on

---

19. See *The Letter on Apologetics and History and Dogma,* trans. Alexander Dru and Illtyd Trethowan (New York: Holt, Rinehart and Winston, 1964), pp. 202–3 and note. This is a worthy concern, the sort of thing that Fechner and James, Whitehead and Hartshorne have insisted upon—but without having to introduce the incarnation to show how God can have sympathy with finite experience.

God's part. His aim must be rather to bring existing potentialities to fruition, guiding them in the direction of "more being," which is also open and adaptable being, more susceptible of further inducements to growth. Rahner and Barth would have to show how a Christocentric universe would differ from other possible universes, and they would have to demonstrate that the present universe fills those specifications. But the task is impossible; there is no difference. Therefore we are left with an "identity of indiscernibles." Although the Christocentrist position may have the advantages of taking a more unified view of the whole process, it has the disadvantage of being nothing more than a speculative "overbelief," going far beyond all connections with the data and treating much too cavalierly the interpretations that are suggested more readily by the data themselves.

In the last analysis the only compelling motive for the Christocentrist position is the one I have hinted at a number of times already: the desire to find some basis of certainty in an uncertain universe, some unconditioned event in the midst of contingency, some definitive and irreversible event, intended from the beginning, in the face of constant change. Such a concern should not be viewed with contempt, for in an open and pluralistic universe, filled with contingencies, theology does confront a new sort of threat: God might appear to be at best a constitutional monarch, depending upon the consent of the governed to put his purposes into effect, and at worst a suppliant in the face of total defeat. The assertions of Christianity both about Jesus and about the eschaton do come into conflict with that kind of total relativism, for which everything flows into an indefinite future, and it might seem plausible, therefore, to give some focus and direction to God's activities by centering everything on the incarnation. Then the contingencies could be acknowledged to the full, but the total process would remain anchored in certain unshakable events.

However understandable the concern, the resolution that is offered does violence to the shape of events as we know them, and a better way can be indicated, although it will require us to engage in some further theological reflection.

2. Divine Purpose in an Open Universe

Let us begin by distinguishing between *intention* and *motivation*. Although we often speak as though they were equivalent, we mean by intention the plan that we have in mind when we act, *what* we are trying to accomplish, while we mean by motivation the volitional impulse that is involved, *why* we are trying to do it; and this "why" is not primarily a value beyond the will which draws it forth, but a modality of the will itself, either a passive affect or an active attitude that is adopted.

One theological tendency, associated with the Scotists, is to think almost entirely in terms of intention, the values that are held in the practical reason, and to seek a proper ranking of God's various "intentions" or "decrees." The reason that the Scotists are called voluntaristic is chiefly that they must give a large role to choice after the pure possibilities have been formulated. But the alternative position is much more profoundly voluntaristic, for it thinks in terms of "motivation," which stays within the framework of the will. This is manifested by the constant statements in traditional theology to the effect that in all God's acts his end, his reason for acting, his motivation, is simply himself, or his own will, or his good pleasure, or his love—that is, the basis of his actions cannot be either a necessity imposed upon him or the positive attraction of some value to be achieved in the world, but it must be simply "because of himself," or "because he willed it," or "out of love."

To affirm this traditional assertion does not preclude the possibility that God's intentions might also involve a subordinate end, a result that is sought outside himself, in the world. This was seen even in the Middle Ages, and since the seventeenth century there has been a steadily growing insistence that God is genuinely concerned with the finite process and seeks its fulfillment (usually termed the *gloria Dei externa*, the outward expression of his glory), perhaps that he even has a stake in the outcome and finds greater joy and enrichment in its success than in its failure.[20] It would seem that this modern concern could be affirmed all the more wholeheartedly by a position which allows God to remain in some respects above the process and not be entirely poured out into it, to remain superior in dignity to anything that is

---

20. For a discussion of the classical debate on this matter within Catholicism, see Philip J. Donnelly, "Saint Thomas and the Ultimate Purpose of Creation," *Theological Studies*, II (1941): 53–83. The distinction is not adequately recognized in the otherwise useful essays in the *Dictionnaire de théologie catholique*, "Fin dernière" by P. Richard (*DTC*, V.2, 2477–2504) and "Création" by H. Pinard (*DTC*, III.2, 2034–2201, esp. 2163–73).

actualized within the finite. Thus we could say that God's motive in creation is his own love or good pleasure, but that the content of his will in creation is to communicate himself to the finite process and bring it to fuller participation in his own perfections, and that he positively seeks this increasing receptivity to himself, this fuller reflection of himself, within the finite.

Such a position may be a more accurate version (from the standpoint of theology's concerns) of what Charles Hartshorne has been championing for many years under the name of "neo-classical" or "dipolar" or "A-R" theism: the view that God's life has both an absolute and a relative pole, the former his eternal and unthreatened being, the latter his genuine relatedness, through knowing and willing, to the finite process. The improvement I am suggesting is that at least some of the language about the "A" pole be translated into terms of motivation, so that God's freedom in love will be one of the ways in which he eternally transcends the world, even in and with his involvement with it. Then even if, for example, one were to say, as Whitehead and Hartshorne do (and as Teilhard strongly hints), that matter or energy always exists alongside God, or, again, that God's acts are conditioned upon what can arise out of the given configurations in the world at any stated time (not that God cannot do something, but, as Aquinas says, that the thing cannot be done, that it is intrinsically impossible), still God's freedom would not be compromised any more than it was in the Plotinian and general patristic view that love is *"diffusivum sui,"* for if there are any necessities or demands or pleas that might come from outside himself, he still transcends them with the freedom of a superabundant love, spontaneous, generous, bringing to the situation more than is demanded and thus retaining freedom of action.

The divine motivation of which I have been speaking, a motivation that transcends the finite process but is not indifferent to it, can best be described by the biblical term *covenant*. Although the origins of this term and the contexts in which it was used will long be a matter of debate among scholars of the ancient Near East, its biblical meaning is clear enough to give us moral certitude about the way to employ it in theology. A covenant involves a commitment or an assumption of responsibility, of the sort expressed by the formula, "I will be your God and you will be my people." It is a kind of relationship which is personal par excellence, for it is based upon a free and knowing decision on the part of a personal agent, giving definite shape to the future where it would otherwise remain indefinite and indeterminate, subject to arbitrary whim. In form it belongs not to the purely religious sphere but to social and political life, where commitments, once made, have to be honored—the marital bond, the commercial agreement, the political treaty (although of course all of these were penetrated by religious sanctions in the ancient world).

A covenant is a freely made commitment to a certain course of action or a certain set of relationships in the future, and its fulfillment is dependent upon the honor and fidelity of the one who makes the commitment. But a covenant, while it gives a definite shape to the future, is not always equivalent with what we speak of as a promise or a contract. A promise is fully specified, and the focus of attention is upon the actions or things being promised; the same applies to a contract between equals. Both of these involve explicitly stated "intentions." But a covenant, although it may be this specific, need not be. It can be more open-ended and undefined, a general commitment to mutual or even unilateral loyalty, heedless of contingencies that might arise. It is more on the side of "motivation," then, a fundamental posture taken by the will. A covenant can have conditions, but these conditions usually take the form of quasi-legal specifications of what each partner must do or refrain from doing, *whatever* the circumstances, and they are most assuredly *not* escape clauses enabling one partner or the other to renege in the face of adversity. Here again we see that the covenant form is intensely personal, a mode of relationship that transcends the accidental and fleeting interactions of physical events and establishes a continuity that is independent of them, although it may also take them into account and adjust to them.

All of this was pointed out long since by one of the first great analysts of Christian language, Anselm,[21] and his discussion concerned precisely the same theme as the present essay. In *Cur Deus Homo?* he wants to say that God is free, and that his decisions are not under constraint by anything outside himself. Yet the whole argument of the work depends upon there being a certain "necessity" for the incarna-

---

21. For this aspect of Anselm's literary activity, see Desmond Paul Henry, *The Logic of Saint Anselm* (Oxford: Oxford University Press, 1967), and the introductory essay in *Truth, Freedom, and Evil: Three Philosophical Dialogues*, ed. and trans. Jasper Hopkins and Herbert Richardson (New York: Harper Torchbooks, 1967).

tion and death of Christ. The resolution, given in book II, chapter 18, is that this necessity is not one imposed upon God but one that arises from his unchanging disposition or purpose respecting man. It can be called necessity; but it is not "antecedent necessity," imposed from outside, but "subsequent necessity," following upon a decision of the agent himself. His point is that the incarnation is necessary only in the sense that God perseveres in his original resolve to bring man to eternal life, acting not out of compulsion but *with the same freedom with which he first made that resolve.* To put it in the terms of our own discussion, a covenant is a commitment freely made, and when it is subsequently followed through there is not a cessation of freedom but a continuation of that same freedom, the free ratification of a commitment freely made in the past. Indeed, without this ongoing exercise of freedom in fidelity to the original commitment the continuity between past and present would become much poorer, for it creates a living continuity, sustained only by the freedom and fidelity of the will. Thus it is an even more sovereign expression of freedom than the *acte gratuit* which has fascinated more than one novelist, for an arbitrary and erratic course through life may turn out merely to be excessively responsive to the changing play of events, while continuity of this sort is an assertion of full and perfect freedom, pursuing a consistent course of action even in the midst of all the vicissitudes that may arise from external circumstances.

In that chapter Anselm applies his analysis of necessity within freedom to something quite specific, namely, the "necessity" of Christ's death because of God's intentions already announced through the prophets. But within the context of the whole work it has a broader import. The overarching argument, it will be recalled, is that the incarnation has a certain antecedent "necessity" such that it can be deduced, so to speak, from other assertions the Christian makes about God. When we look at the argument not in terms of the particular theory of atonement that Anselm sets up in book I of *Cur Deus Homo?* but in terms of the sketch of the history of salvation that he gives in book II, we find a simple and quite convincing statement of God's fundamental resolve or commitment and the "necessities" that grow from it. Anselm begins with the standard assumption of Christian doctrine that God created rational beings to love him for his own sake and to find happiness in the enjoyment of him, and that men, if they had allowed this purpose to bear fruit in their lives, would have been brought to eternal happiness without experiencing death, the tearing away of the body from the soul. This is God's original commitment. But they have sinned —freely, not through divine foreordination. If God is to complete what he has begun and not see his original purpose frustrated completely, it is "necessary" that he effect salvation for them, although of course this "necessity" is only the consistent maintenance of a purpose already decided upon (II, 4–5).

Here we have it: God makes a commitment which is not restricted to any one scenario, not conditioned upon the playing out of a particular sequence of events, which is, then, broader and deeper than all the contingencies that may arise, but which can also take those contingencies into account, adjust to them, make new moves in the face of seeming frustrations. If it is really to take them into account, it must remain indeterminate with respect to the details and not be pinned irrevocably to any of them, although this is quite consistent with a perfect definiteness about the commitment that is being made and the general direction to be taken.

When we ask what is the fundamental commitment God makes, the one that animates all his particular decisions and gives continuity to his actions, we find that the farther back we move the more indeterminate it must be. From the perspective of the Christian Church, telescoping everything into one vision of the whole, it is the person and the continuing lordship of Christ; but from the perspective of Israel, it is the fulfillment of the promises and hopes recorded in the Scriptures; from the perspective of a sinful humanity generally, deliverance from bondage to sin and decay and transiency (and we need not assume that these earlier insights are ever superseded, that they ever become irrelevant); from the perspective of the first stirrings of human life, a profitable rather than an unprofitable career for the human race under the sponsorship of God's gracious presence; from the perspective of an evolving phylum of vertebrates, the rise of a being capable of response to God; from the perspective of a cosmos in its incipient stages, the enhancement of diversity so that it will give the maximum opportunities for evolution toward beings that will reflect with increasing accuracy the perfection of God's being.

But however indeterminate the content of God's purposes becomes as we move back, there is no obstacle to our saying that he makes a commitment of a certain kind from the beginning, and that it is deployed, with increasingly more determinateness but always in a way faithful to the original purpose, in the course of time. Indeed, the end may join itself in a curious way to the beginning; for if the end is a union of creatures with God through knowledge and love, then the formal conditions for that state of affairs could have been outlined from the beginning (omitting, that is, any exact indication of the biological and historical path to be taken toward the goal). The clue, then, would be not Christology as such, but eschatology. This focusing upon eschatology is not based on current theological fashion, or on a desire to hide the key that unlocks all secrets in a place that cannot come under scrutiny from profane knowledge; it follows from the nature of the case, for the real *eschaton* is God himself, to whom finite life, it is hoped, will eventually return. This *eschaton* can be present from the beginning—Omega is also Alpha—and the essential features of the union of finite and infinite can be outlined when it is nothing more than a vague potentiality on the part of matter and a firm but still open and indeterminate purpose on the part of God.

This, I take it, is what Karl Rahner really means (or ought to mean) when he speaks of God's first and comprehensive decision as being his self-impartation or self-communication to that which is other than himself. Such language, although it is derived from the tradition of participationist metaphysics, is equivalent to the biblical language of covenant, for in both cases what is meant is a spontaneous and generous commitment on God's part, a decision, as Barth likes to put it, not to be God by himself but to be God with and for the other. The more philosophical language of self-impartation adds something, however, to the narrowly "moral" or "mental" or "intentional" language of covenant by suggesting that a "real" change is involved, that God makes himself present in his own heart and his own being, with all his sustaining and directing power, and thus makes himself the most important factor in the situation of every finite thing. But the biblical language of covenant also adds something to the philosophical discussion of creation as participation, for it suggests that God's creative influence is always personal, that he is present not merely as enabling or grounding the evolutionary process but as polarizing it in a definite direction, with a broad purpose that at any given time reaches out beyond the current potentialities or strivings within the finite world, and with a freedom of decision that is repeatedly brought to bear upon the changing course of events. In this way—through his own *being* as God, focused, by his own good pleasure, upon the good of the created world through his *covenant*—God constitutes the one sufficient guarantee of the success of the whole process, and the guarantee as well of its fulfilling his initial purpose despite the erratic path it may follow and the number of corrective measures that must be taken.

So much for the basic purpose that animates the process, the covenant that is faithfully carried out from beginning to end and thereby guarantees its own fulfillment. All of this attests to God's transcendence of the world. But what ought to be said about the character of God's involvement with the process, his interaction with the actual course of events, the deployment of his purpose in definite acts?

We should begin, perhaps, with the parable in the book of the prophet Jeremiah, chapter 18. Jeremiah has been told to go and watch the potter working at his wheel. He notices that when the vessel the potter is making is spoiled in some way, perhaps by a slip of the hand, or if the clay will not work up properly into the vessel he had planned, he does not knead the clay back into a lump and start over but *reworks* it into another kind of vessel, according to what seems best to his practiced eye. Then the Word of the Lord comes to Jeremiah:

> O house of Israel, can I not do with you as this potter has done? says the Lord.
> Behold, like the clay in the potter's hand, so are you in my hand . . . .
> (18:6)

But the point is not that God manipulates the destinies of men, as though they were merely "clay in his hand." It is just the opposite:

> If at any time I declare concerning a nation or a kingdom, that I will pluck up and break down and destroy it, and if that nation . . . turns from its evil, I will repent of the evil that I intended to do to it. And if at any time I declare concerning a nation or a kingdom that I will build and plant it, and if it does evil in my sight, not listening to my voice, then I will repent of the good which I had intended to do to it. (18:7–10)

The comparison is thus intended to show the *plasticity* of God's plans, their flexibility and adaptability. God takes human actions into account as he makes his plans, like a skilled craftsman who knows his materials and adjusts his purposes in keeping with them. Then comes the application:

> "Thus says the Lord, Behold, I am shaping evil against you and devising a plan against you. Return, every one from his evil way, and amend your ways and your doings." (18:11)

The Word of the Lord does not foreclose the future and abolish human freedom, even when it comes in the form of threat or promise; rather it intensifies freedom by presenting alternatives to man and requiring of him a decision which will then affect his destiny and the subsequent attitude of God toward him.

Theologians have long been bothered by the consequences of this undeniably biblical (or at least Israelite) understanding of God, for it suggests that God's plans may be held open for a time pending man's decision, and even that God's announced intentions may be frustrated by an adverse decision on man's part. So we find, on the one hand, that they have taken an interest in analyzing the biblical language about God's willing. They have known the difference between God's effective will, by which he takes direct responsibility for events, his approving will, by which he concurs in what is performed by others, and his permitting will, by which he allows evil to occur without in any way approving it. They have also known that we can speak of "God's will" when we mean not an act of willing directed toward actual events in the world (whether to do them, or approve them, or merely to permit them) but an act of willing that is expressed in the form of commands, exhortations, promises, threats, and the like, what the scholastics called God's "*voluntas signi.*" But at the same time they have attempted to blunt the force of these analyses, for they knew that if God's commanding and promising and threatening will is a reliable reflection of his own intentions, it means that God really desires or promises or threatens something that in fact will never occur; and this seemed to them incompatible with God's perfection, which ought to be free of such frustrations. Therefore they asserted that his knowing and willing are timeless, for this alone could keep him from commanding or promising something that would never be fulfilled; and they asserted in addition that God's publicly expressed willing (the *voluntas signi*) is *not* a reliable reflection of his definitive willing, the willing whose object is the actual course of events (God's *voluntas beneplaciti*). This meant that there could be no genuine interaction between God and men, that the many promises and threats which remained unfulfilled had to be viewed as mere stratagems on God's part to maneuver them into the position where he wanted them, that prayer could not really change God's mind concerning anything although, again, it was useful for them and one of the means God had eternally willed for the accomplishment of his definitive will. All of this, although it was drawn into a coherent and often impressive system, is inconsistent with the plain sense of many writings in the Bible (though not of all) and with the understanding of God that they are obviously expressing. Since the Bible does not speak with one voice on this matter (it scarcely does on any), we must make normative judgments on our own responsibility, and I have been arguing that the only satisfactory position, for many reasons, is the one that would take seriously a temporal unfolding of God's purposes and would acknowledge that they might not—could not —be complete in every detail from the beginning.

What we must affirm, then, is a basic policy decision on God's part, what we have called, in biblical fashion, the covenant, his self-committal to drawing the world toward the most intimate and intense union with himself—but also the constant adjustment of this policy in keeping with changing circumstances. From the perspective of the Christian faith and its existential concerns, there are three basic deployments of this policy: *creation*, the decision to begin structuring the chaotic flow of energy in certain ways, with a view to its higher development; *grace*, God's decision, once man has arisen, to lead him toward himself and assist him on the way; and *salvation*, the decision, once man has sinned, to remain faithful to this original intention, not withdrawing his gracious presence to human life but continuing it, now not only for the sake of fellowship between God and man but for the overcoming of man's rebellion, and consenting to count man righteous if his fundamental commitment is appropriate, even though he never overcomes temptation completely.

But how are we to deal with such classic problems as the possibility of salvation before or outside the Christian Church, the relation of the Old Testament to the New, the Messianic anticipations in the Old Testament, and the like? The traditional view, of course (assumed in the New Testament itself and in all subsequent exegesis until the rise of strict historical scholarship), was that the Old Testament was to be interpreted from the New, since the promises and the foreshadowings recorded there, however obsure their message and unsure their reference, directly envisaged the coming of Christ. This was quite in keeping with the general assumption that God's knowledge is timeless and that his purposes are completely filled in. But historical study of the meaning of those passages has indicated that, while most of them are indeed Messianic or at least look toward a better future, their meaning is usually linked very closely with the situation and the assumptions of the time of writing and can be made to refer to Jesus of Nazareth only by doing violence to all the evidence. When we add to this the need to take a rather different view of God's relation to the temporal process, we must conclude that the promises and foreshadowings of the Messiah or the Messianic age, insofar as they can be viewed as a valid expression of God's purposes in human words or actions, are rather more *indefinite* and *variegated* than it was formerly supposed, and that their indefiniteness or variety of reference and content is not merely apparent but real. Their sometimes striking correspondence with what subsequently came into being with Jesus of Nazareth is to be explained, then, as the result not of direct prediction (by either man or God) but of a continuity between earlier and later stages of what remains, after all, a unified drama played out between the same God, having the same overarching purposes, and the same people of God, carrying forward and developing the same general understanding of God and the same expressions of his will. With such real continuities, the similarities are not surprising, and the later stages can be taken to be the full unfolding of what was already present, though in a less explicit way, much earlier.

All this will mean that we must not interpret the Old Testament on the basis of the New, but, if anything, the New on the basis of the Old, as more in keeping with the historical facts and with theological reflection. How, then, is it possible for the Christian to keep everything solidly focused upon Jesus as the fulfillment of God's purposes? It should be said first of all that it might be salutary for the Christian to struggle with a problem like this for a while, since he has probably been operating with excessive triumphalism and ought to be taught a sharp lesson, if need be, in humility. But an answer is forthcoming, and it is not a new one, either.

Let us take one of the oldest and clearest and most provocative statements, coming from Augustine: "The very same thing that is now called the Christian religion," he says, "was also among the ancients, and it has never been absent, from the beginning of the human race until Christ came in the flesh, after which time the true religion, which had always been present, began to be called Christian" (*Retr.*, I, 12, 3; cf. also *Ep.* 102, q. 2, 11–12). This is, of course the premise of his sketch of the earthly history of the City of God, beginning with Abel and other righteous men. Although he thinks that this salvation is available in some way everywhere, he also knows the importance of earthly revelations and rituals and institutions, and this is the singular virtue of the heritage of Israel and the Church. It is in the context of this theme —the availability of the same salvation before Christianity, but the importance of earthly symbols all the same—that we must understand his doctrine that what is "latent" in the Old Testament becomes "patent" in the New (*De pecc. orig.*, II, 24, 29–30, 35; *De nupt. et conc.*, II, 11, 24; III 4, 7–13; *De civ. Dei*, XVIII, 47). Its purpose is *not* primarily to set up an opposition between them (although of course he asserts that the New Testament is clearer than the Old), or even to relate them as promise and fulfillment, but to offer an explanation for his assertion that *one and the same covenant and promise and salvation* can be conveyed to people in different times, despite the obvious differences in rituals and symbols.

Warrant for this is found, of course, in those passages where Paul asserts that Abraham is the father of all believers (Romans 4); where he points out that the Torah, with all that seemingly sets Jews and Gentiles at odds with each other, came 430 years, by his reckoning, after the promise to Abraham and must be interpreted within the context of the promise (Galatians 3); where he suggests that the passage through the Red Sea, and the eating of manna, and the drinking of water from the rock, were a kind of sacramental participation in the same salvation that is offered in Christ (1 Corinthians 10); where he says that Israel, the people of the promise, was and remains elect as a people (Romans 9–11).[22] It is something that the Church easily forgot

22. Cf. *Franz Rosenzweig: His Life and Thought,* presented by Nahum N. Glatzer (second edition; New York: Schocken Books, 1961), p. 341, from a letter to Rudolf Ehrenburg shortly after Rosenzweig's decision to remain a Jew: "We are wholly agreed as to what Christ and his church mean to the world: no one can

once it became almost exclusively Gentile; but from time to time the problem was brought forcibly to its attention by the Gnostics, and then the Marcionites, and finally the Manichaeans, groups which were ready enough to view Christ as the Redeemer but which set up an opposition between him and the deity of the Old Testament.

In a long section of the *Institutes* (II, 9–11) Calvin develops this theme. There is one covenant, he says, in different "modes of administration" (II, 10, 2; 11, 1). The difference in modes of administration is, quite simply, the difference between a preparatory stage in which people are led, like children, through written laws and external ceremonies, embedded in the ethos of a single nation, sanctioned by political enforcement and hopes of an earthly reward—and a stage of fulfillment, in which they are brought to maturity and freedom, and the same offer is opened to all nations, and their hope trandscends earth (II, 11). But such a contrast, he thinks, taken by itself, is misleading; it must be understood from the first within the fundamental identity of the two dispensations, and then the seeming opposition becomes instead a positive correspondence between the two. In Calvin's actual discussion of the matter it comes down to two particular problems. One is the difference in rituals or sacraments; and here he affirms that their "signification" is actually the same in both cases, although it is more explicit in the New Testament (II, 10, 5–6). The other is the striking difference between the Old Testament hope for earthly rewards and the New Testament hope for eternal life; and here Calvin argues that those promises of earthly prosperity were always a kind of code-sign which really conveyed a promise of everlasting happiness with God (II, 10, 7–23), a mirror in which they could contemplate their future inheritance (II, 11, 1), and that the patriarchs and other righteous persons were allowed to understand this by the inward illumination of the Word (II, 10, 7). And he reminds those Christians who take too triumphalist an attitude toward the Christian life and set it in opposition to Judaism that they also must walk by faith in the promises of Christ, still at a distance from the goal (II, 9, 3).

Knowing what we do today as a result of historical studies we find it

---

reach the Father save through him. No one can reach the Father! But the situation is quite different for one who does not have to reach the Father because he is already with him. And this is true of the people of Israel (though not of individual Jews)."

impossible to say it in precisely this way. There is no indication of such a hope for life after death in most of the Hebrew Scriptures, and although there was a belief in "survival" in Sheol (attested most dramatically in the story of Saul's visit to the witch of Endor), this was not the object of a positive religious hope—unless perhaps Enoch and Elijah are to be taken as more than exceptions to the rule. Yet Calvin's case is not so shaky as it might appear. He himself is aware of the difficulties of interpreting the Hebrew Scriptures as a testimony to Christian salvation, and he does not rely entirely on the *deus ex machina* of inspiration but engages in some hard-headed analysis of the problem. The real justification for pressing beyond the apparent meaning of the promises made to the men of the Old Testament is the stark contrast between what was promised to them and the actual condition of earthly life, of which they knew all too well. Abraham, Isaac, and Jacob, despite the promises made to them, never acquired a foot of land in Canaan except for their own graves (III, 10, 13), and it was known to David and others that God rarely or never gives to his servants, in this world, the things he promises them (II, 10, 17). Similarly it is almost impossible to expect the realization in earthly life of many of the things mentioned by the prophets (II, 10, 20). With such frank observations on the human condition Calvin arrives at his guidelines for interpreting the real import of biblical hopes.[23]

What Calvin has done, if we put it in the vocabulary of modern historical studies, is to give an accurate characterization of the claims and aspirations that run throughout Israelite religion and eventually lead to the rise of prophetic eschatology and then apocalyptic. The scope of Israel's faith in God, the reach of its hopes, are so broad that they cannot be entirely satisfied with the earthly present, and when disappointments become intense enough this trust and this hope must be projected beyond earth altogether. ("These all died in faith, not having received what was promised, but having seen it and greeted it from afar, and having acknowledged that they were strangers and exiles on

23. Ian D. K. Siggins, *Martin Luther's Doctrine of Christ* (New Haven: Yale University Press, 1970), pp. 24–26, has pointed out a similar pattern of interpretation in Luther's commentary on the Minor Prophets (1525–27). There Luther calls the method *"transitus"* (= Passover), a going over from the apparent meaning, which is full of impossibilities and inconsistencies, to the meaning which has always been the real one, the fulfillment of all these promises in Christ. Note should also be taken of Pascal's arguments from prophecy in his draft of an "apology for the true religion" (*Pensées*, #382 and #394).

the earth" [Heb. 11:13].) Here we have the proper "hermeneutic" of
the Hebrew Scriptures, one that is not an arbitrarily imposed Christian
hermeneutic but can be called just as well a Pharisaic hermeneutic,
and which is firmly rooted in the actual historical development of
Israel's religion. This is the reason for all midrashic and allegorical exegesis, the sense that Scripture somehow conveys more than it seems to
say on the surface and that inconsistencies or impossibilities may be a
sign that there is more to be looked for. In our day we know better
how to resist the tendency of the rabbis and the fathers to make Scripture conform to and reinforce their prior assumptions; but our own
procedure is much the same when we try to understand the basic drift
of a writing, its unexpressed assumptions, the interest that animates it,
the horizon of its vision, its further implications, and in the process discover that its import is rather different than it first appeared.

When we view the matter in this way perhaps we can say after all
that the spirituality of ancient Israel, and of subsequent Judaism, is
fundamentally the same as that of Christianity, that what is proclaimed
in Christianity with an air of finality and certitude is already proclaimed there with somewhat more tentativeness and expectancy.
While it is good to have finality (for it is the sign of an actualization of
what had been only hoped for), it never entirely supersedes the phase
of expectancy. In all practical affairs, at least, the possibility precedes
the actuality and continues to give it definiteness, the striving precedes
the fruition and continues to give it relevance.

If the spirituality of Israel is fundamentally identical with that of the
Church, if what is "patent" in the latter is already "latent" in the
former, how are we to *explain* this phenomenon? How is it that a
vague longing can be essentially the same as a sense of having found?
Not, certainly, through any sharing of the same real *object,* for what is
explicit in the later faith is merely implicit, if even that, in the earlier.
The equivalence must be on the side of the subject, in the orientation
and the modality of its concerns and in the experiences that have given
rise to them. Then they can mount to greater explicitness and subside
again, be verbalized in legal demands and symbolized in images of
future states of affairs, and perhaps find illustration in persons and
events that satisfy (completely or to some degree) their longings; but
throughout all these changes the orientation can remain the same and
be rooted in the same basic experience.

Some will recognize the similarity of these statements to an analysis of human consciousness that has been widespread among modern Catholic thinkers who are concerned with the nature of belief and its development through time, among whom should be mentioned, as the most creative and influential, Newman, Blondel, and Rahner.[24] Rahner in particular has extrapolated from the character of doctrinal developments within Christianity to a more generalized theory of the dynamics of religious life.[25] As he presents it (and here our argument converges with his position) the situation of all is affected by the presence of the gracious God, inviting men to communion with himself and, when sin arises, offering them the possibility of salvation out of faithfulness to his original purpose. The problem, of course, is how this gracious presence of God can make a real difference to them even where it is not proclaimed in so many words; and his answer is that it somehow makes itself known or felt in their inmost being, whether they are explicitly conscious of it or not, and whether they respond to it or do not. Only this explains how there can be "anonymous Christians" potentially anywhere in human history—among primitive peoples, ancient Hebrews and modern Jews, pagan scoffers, sectarian and deviationist Christians, post-Christian despisers of religion—as long as they respond favorably to this secret influence of the gracious God. (If the expression "anonymous Christianity" seems offensive, one might follow Augustine's practice and simply call it "true religion," reserving the name of Christianity to the particular historical movement. But by whatever name he calls it, Rahner knows that he must follow the standard of Christian belief that salvation is *not* possible on the basis of virtue alone, or doing one's best according to one's lights, or having good intentions; there must be an actual dependence on the saving grace of God and at least the beginnings of an actual transformation of life.) People can have an implicit faith even though their beliefs and actions seem quite different from the doctrinal and institutional forms sponsored by the Church, for there is always a difference between the

---

24. For Newman, see especially *Oxford University Sermons*, sermons XIV and XV, and *An Essay on the Development of Christian Doctrine*, chaps. I and II; for Blondel, *History and Dogma*, sec. iii, esp. pp. 267–76; for Rahner, *Theological Investigations*, I, 39–78; IV, 3–35.

25. For a more extensive discussion of this theme and its place in Rahner's entire theology, see William C. Shepherd, *Man's Condition: God and the World Process* (New York: Herder & Herder, 1969).

inward attitudes and commitments with which one enacts his life and the symbolizations by which he tries to bring them to expression. In any cultural or religious community a multitude of ideas will be in circulation, and one who has responded to grace will discriminate among them with sure instincts, for the *Gestalt* of his central assumptions will be right—and, on the other hand, someone who appears outwardly to be an orthodox Catholic may be inwardly sterile or corrupt.[26]

The universal possibility of salvation does not make doctrinal and institutional forms any less important, for human life is never enacted in complete privacy, apart from concrete circumstances and interpretative schemata and ritual patterns, and Rahner thinks that it is in the Christian community that this largely implicit faith "comes to itself" in explicit formulation. Although the saving grace of God is present everywhere in human history, there is a "history of salvation" in the full sense only where this saving grace is expressed in words and institutions, gaining an intra-mundane, sensory "presence" and thus encountering us unavoidably within our day-to-day sphere of operation. Rahner interprets the incarnation within the same framework, as the succession of acts in which God's grace comes to full expression within the world and as a result becomes irreversibly present to human history, as mediated, of course, through the sacraments and teaching activity of the Church.

Unfortunately Rahner has not been willing to grant an unqualified validity to the expressions of grace and salvation in the life of Israel. Here he seems to be influenced by the longstanding indifference of Teutonic culture toward the Jews and by a tradition of biblical interpretation which has stressed the incompleteness and inadequacy of the Old Testament. His own principles would seem to require a much more positive evaluation of this phase of the history of salvation, a phase in which, at the very least, the requirements and goals were marked out and the lack of fulfillment in human life was acknowledged courageously—and in which the reality of redemption is also attested in sanctified lives.

Despite such occasional instances of shortsightedness, Rahner does

26. See especially "Christianity and the Non-Christian Religions," *Theological Investigations,* V, 115–35, and, on the other side, the hard-hitting essay "What Is Heresy?" pp. 468–512 in the same volume.

offer the framework for a broader view of salvation than do most Christian theologies. The consequences of his theory of the omnipresence of grace, taken to their full extent, are precisely the opposite of what Rahner himself suggests: it is not that everything must be organized around the one figure of Jesus, but that Jesus is the complete and definitive expression of a relationship between God and man which is present, at least in potentiality, from the very first and which can be acknowledged and approximated to some degree at any time and place.

This brings us, by a different route, to the topics that have been discussed in Chapters I and II—the Pauline doctrine of the New Adam as in some sense a manifestation of man as the "image of God" and its philosophical transformation in the motif of the "archetypal ideal" of humanity. We are in a position to resume those earlier inquiries, asking how the mythic "primal man" or the philosophical "ideal of humanity" can best be understood from the perspective of a theology oriented to open, evolving world.

3. The Context of Christology

If we take seriously the converging indications that God's purposes are not fully defined from eternity but grow in precision as he knows the actual course of events and adapts his will accordingly, then we will *not* expect to find everything focused upon Christ, or even upon the "human race" as we know it empirically, and we will look for overarching unity *not* in a detailed divine plan but in the transcendent being of God as he draws the finite process toward fuller participation in his own perfection; and once the human race appears we will find, again, a genuine development that moves from indeterminacy toward definiteness.

Abundant proof has been given here, I trust, that such a perspective cannot be considered disastrous to theology, since it has fundamental similarities with a style of thinking expressed by theologians more or less continuously through many centuries. The point they have in common, as I have just suggested, is that they seek a basis of unity not in an empirical individual but in God as transcending all that is or will be within the finite. This means that, when we come to human life, its unity in God's purposes can be stated along lines similar to those marked out in the classic notion of an "ideal" of humanity, for it is in terms of this "ideal," variously conceived, that theology has recurrently discussed the place of Christ. Even if we allow for a growing precision and a repeated adjustment of God's plans, and for constant historical change in man's own moral and speculative and religious apprehensions, we cannot afford to dispense with some such notion. (What I am concerned with is chiefly its *function* in theological reflection, for it is, quite simply, the correlate, on the divine side, of human intelligence and freedom. Once human life is on the scene there will be, at least implicitly or covertly, a question about the ends it will seek, the character of its fulfillment, the destiny to which it is called). The destiny need not be innately known, or be discoverable by pure reason (we should expect, rather, to find it in the encounter between God and man). Still it will be pertinent to human life, first, perhaps, only as a question, as an unknown and merely postulated "function," and then as a call to be acknowledged.

This is the anthropological and theological space—man concerned with God, God concerned with man—in terms of which Christology must be understood. In the language of traditional Christology, the priority must lie with the divine Word, for this is where the "ideal" for humanity—God's purpose, covenant, call—is conceptualized and developed. The humanity of Jesus, although it is shaped by and attests to the Word, neither exhausts the Word nor is the sole means of access to it, for the Word is both knowable and efficacious elsewhere. The uniqueness of Jesus—a uniqueness which should not be seen apart from the uniqueness of Israel and the Church—will consist, then, in being the touchstone by which other responses are judged, the achievement by which their deficiencies are overcome, the center of gravity around which they cluster.

Since the primary horizon of concern is this encounter of divine covenant with human freedom, we should not be surprised to see it played out in the different modalities that I earlier linked with the three articles of the Creed, noting again that these modalities are based not on the Trinity but on the aspects of human life in the economy of salvation. First—and always—the divine call makes us aware of our freedom and points to the parting of the ways between good and evil, response and failure. Indeed, it shows us, without mitigating our sense of responsibility, that we are already somewhere along the way of failure. But we can also find our attention drawn to what Paul called the warfare between flesh and Spirit, between the continuing effects of sin and a new power of salvation in dependence upon another. We can even have confidence that we share in an ultimate fulfillment, despite all our frustrations. Let us consider these three aspects once again in order to see what they can tell us about God, man, and Christ.

The theme of what Rahner calls "anonymous Christianity"—it could better be called "true religion" or "man under grace"—belongs with the theology of the first article that was explored by Kant and Schelling. Like Kant, Rahner begins with the general human situation and views Christ and Christianity as, from one perspective, the manifestation of a possibility that is in principle present everywhere and, from another perspective, as an indispensable vehicle for its being known and shared publicly and fully actualized. Like Schelling he is prepared to see in all religions at least some scattered reflections of a universal presence and revelation of God. The difference, of course, is that Rahner understands this universal revelation and the possibilities for human life that arise from it as *grace*, the presence of God inviting men into communion with himself and maintaining this invitation despite the fact of sin.

But something can still be learned, I think, from those earlier reflections on the problem, since they suggest more explicitly that this divine grace or self-impartation can never become domesticated to human life, does not become fully ingredient in it; the divine transcendence of this grace is manifested in the form of law or promise, always hovering above man. One of the most notable features of the thought of Kant and of Schelling, as we saw, is their insistence that the practical "ideal" or creative "idea" of true humanity continues to transcend the actual condition of man, both on the metaphysical grounds that the temporal can never be fully adequate to the eternal and on the moral grounds that the human will as we find it never attains to holiness. In Kant in particular this distance between the ideal and the reality helps to reinforce and explain not only the eschatological striving for the perfection of the kingdom of God, but the continuing sense of guilt and (simultaneously) the possibility of justification where the fundamental aspirations are right. This, I suggest, offers an important corrective to what Rahner says about the general possibility of salvation, for he scarcely takes note of the temptations and struggles, the feelings of inadequacy and guilt which, if they are part of Christian experience, *a fortiori* must be part of the experience of his "anonymous Christian." To say that the gracious God is everywhere present and makes himself felt in the human mind and heart, and that men may respond to him, is not to say that their response will fully satisfy either the terms of the call or their own conscience. The addition of this proviso corrects and completes, therefore, Rahner's theory of the anonymous Christian, or Augustine's and Calvin's theory that the same grace is operative in Israel (and elsewhere) as in the Church, for it explains how the reception of saving grace could lead not to tranquility and happiness but to discontent and a striving after something better, how the latter experiences are signs that grace has taken hold, how such experiences are not unfamiliar even to the Christian.

But for precisely this reason the possibility of an "anonymous Christianity" does not make Christ himself superfluous. It causes no difficulty to grant that Christ can be described in terms of a general human possibility which can be favorably responded to apart from him, or that he functions as the "vehicle" (if one cares to use Kant's term) by which it comes to be more widely known and more nearly actualized in others. The real problem is this abiding sense of dissatisfaction and disability, and because of it there is a place for a sense of dependence upon other events, other personages, in which something better has been accomplished. Schleiermacher and others after him have evoked this sense of dependence upon Jesus, as proclaimed by the Christian community, in an especially emphatic way, always linking the experience, it will be noted, to an awareness of continuing failure and guilt and inadequacy. But Jesus need not even have a total monopoly on the events in which evil has been overcome and a responsive obedience hews out a place for itself: one thinks of the many prophets and righteous ones in Israel, mentioned in the teachings of Jesus himself, who were a sign to their generations, though often only as an occasion of stumbling; or the martyrs and saints who came to be venerated because it was felt that the direction of their lives somehow supplemented one's own; or even the moments of testing, of victory or, just as often, of defeat which are remembered by every nation and every ideological group as giving it identity and separating it from what it does not want to be. The fact that there are parallels, even in secular life, does not detract from the Christian understanding of redemption but indicates, if anything, its relevance to potentially all situations and all aspects of life, proving that we do not live merely with a view to ideal possibilities, and neither do we rely upon our own solitary decisions to bring them to fulfillment. We not only depend upon the already completed history of the race in a general way, but often we find past events entering into our consciousness as a source of strength and as a basis for abjuring temptations which might otherwise carry us away.

For these reasons, then, the sense of continued dependence upon Jesus and the need for "mystical incorporation" into him through Christian words and symbols, which we saw was characteristic of Schleiermacher, must be added to the theme of justification which was more characteristic of Kant. If Jesus can be considered unique in this "history of salvation" in that he is experienced as "archetypal," as the New Adam, he can be called this only because he belongs fully to the human race in all its concreteness, closing the gap between the divine call and the human response—not statically, however, so that he becomes a sacred object, but as one who was still "on the way," participating in and overcoming temptation, manifesting concern for his companions, bringing the divine call fully into relation with concrete human situations.

Yet we must also add the insistence (associated especially with the Fourth Gospel, and in modern times with Hegel) that, despite the limitations of human life, there can be at least the beginnings of fulfillment—but only in the medium of inwardness, with its attention directed not toward the earthly or historical aspect of any event, but toward the divine realm into which it is taken up once again and where all the riches of the divine Spirit can be shared by the human spirit. For Hegel this fulfillment was an outgrowth of the historical tradition of Christianity. But the experience, I suspect, can also be traced elsewhere, not only in Vedanta and other forms of mysticism which overleap the historical altogether, but (most astounding from the standpoint of Christian prejudices) in Judaism after the expulsion from Spain, when Cabbalists and Hasidic *rebbe's* began to feel that Israel had received double for her sins (at the very least!), and instead of passively awaiting the days of the Messiah they began to discern the dawning of an eschatological fulfillment in the spiritual fervor of devoted men and women and tried to hasten its coming through their own work and worship.

What such phenomena indicate is that, if there is not a development *beyond* Jesus, at least there is the possibility of the same communion with God—and in the modality not merely of hope but of fulfillment—*outside* him. They should enable the Christian, perhaps for the first time, to take an unfanatical view of his own faith and its affirmations, and an uncondescending view of the faith of others—ancient and modern Israel, the other "higher religions" of the world, the "indigenous religions," even the concerns of the morally sensitive and the committed, whoever they may be—without diminishing the vigor of his own affirmations and commitments. Of course the way the Christian phrases it may not please others, and they will want to say it in their own way, granting, one would hope, to the Christian the same privilege that they claim for themselves, to take a particular point of view in describing the human situation. But what is of chief importance here is to approach all people in a spirit of openness and generosity, for a self-esteem that is purchased through deprecation or contempt of others and cannot be maintained in honest encounter with them is not worth having.

There is a sociological lesson to be drawn here. It may not be a coincidence that Christocentrism was not seriously entertained until after the triumph of Christianity in Western culture, indeed, not until after its position began to be threatened, not until after theologians had lost confidence in the ability of reason and experience to mediate between believers and non-believers, not until after the Church had begun to meet the increasing independence of secular life with exaggerated claims and overambitious power plays. Similarly it may not be a coincidence that the alternative position thrived as long as there was a situation of open encounter, in which one's claims had to be made good in the forum of reason even when it was clear that reason did not solve all problems, in which the gap between potentiality and actuality, demand and fulfillment, had to be closed by decision and enactment. This was the apologetic situation in the patristic age, when there were many philosophers and well-meaning pagans who agreed with the standards and goals taught by the Church, and the real question was where those standards were being taken seriously and those goals being approximated. It is also the situation today, when the Christian West and a Christian America, to the extent that they ever existed, have perished or at best remain an empty illusion. We have begun to see clearly that the Christian message will be advanced not by pretending that all people are Christians and sneaking them into the fold against their wishes, but by taking seriously every authentic human task and learning to talk the same language and consider the same difficulties and the same evidence as everyone else, and making the criterion of success not the number of adherents but the intellectual honesty and moral courage with which we operate, for these can gain respect even when in the end they turn sorrowfully away.

For it should be said, as the last word, that however open and indeterminate we may think God's purposes antecedent to the actual course of evolution and history to have been, and however broad and flexible we may think his continuing relationship toward men and women to be, the definiteness of the Christian commitment and the Christian hope is not compromised. As I have expressed it earlier in this essay, even if one is not a Christocentrist backward, thinking about God's original purposes, one may be a Christocentrist forward, looking to what Teilhard calls the axis along which the greatest progress toward the consummation of all things will be made. If indeterminacy once prevailed in God's purposes, it need not always be so; and if God continues to invite all people into fellowship with himself, this does not hinder the coalescence of human life around points of greater intensity and lines of greater force. There may be other strands of development as well, with varying degrees of potency; but if they are reflections of the same divine influence, then the one vast tide bearing all of human life along can be expected to lead them to converge with the more explicit axis of development in Christ, either in the course of earthly history or, if there is never any such merger, then at the end when he delivers up the kingdom and God is all in all.

Index

I. Scripture References

Genesis
1:27 – 12
3 – 99
3:5 – 20
3:15 – 33
3:21 – 38
3:22 – 20

Exodus
34 – 13
34:34 – 15

Psalms
8:7 – 13
110:1 – 13

Proverbs
8:22 – 35-36

Jeremiah
18 – 153-54

Wisdom of Solomon
5 – 19 n
7 – 33
18 – 19 n

John
1 – 33

Romans
1:18-23 – 9
4 – 157
5:12-21 – 9-10
7 – 62

7:8 – 71
8 – 62
8:3 – 23
8:17 – 13
8:19-23 – 13
8:29 – 12. 13
9-11 – 157
15:3 – 23

1 Corinthians
2:6-13 – 2
10 – 157
11:7 – 12
15 – 10-11
15:20, 23 – 13
15:24 – 25
15:25-27 – 13
15:28 – 13
15:49 – 12, 25

2 Corinthians
3:1-4:6 – 13-16
3:18 – 12
4:3-4 – 24
4:4 – 13
5:6 – 14
8:9 – 23
11:4 – 14
11:5 – 14
11:22 – 14

Galatians
1:10-17 – 16

3 – 157
3:1-4 – 16
4:19 – 12
6:15 – 11

Ephesians
1:9-10 – 27 n, 28
5:31-32 – 39

Philippians
2:1-4 – 23
2:5-11 – 16-23, 24
3:7-11 – 23-24
3:21 – 12

Colossians
1 – 33
1:15 – 12 n
1:15-17 – 36

1 Timothy
2:5 – 24

Hebrews
1 – 33
2:5-9 – 13, 22 n
4:3-11 – 22 n
6:13 – 102
9:26 – 22 n
11:13 – 159-60

Barnabas
6:19 – 22 n
15:6-7 – 22 n

171

2. Names and Subjects